How to Buy Your First Boat

Captain Rami Geffner MD

PAGE PUBLISHING
Conneaut Lake, PA

First originally published by Page Publishing 2024

ISBN 979-8-89315-354-5 (pbk)
ISBN 979-8-89315-367-5 (digital)

Printed in the United States of America

Disclaimer

In no event shall Rami Geffner or any entity associated with him, be liable for any indirect, incidental, special exemplary, or consequential damages (including, but not limited to, procurement of substitute goods or services; loss of use, data, assets or profits; or business interruptions) however caused and on any theory of liability, whether in contract, strict liability or tort (including negligence or otherwise) arising in any way out of the use of this book or its product, even if advised of the possibility of such damage.

Contents

Acknowledgments

Having people support your passion is indeed a blessing. I would not have been able to write this book without the help of some extraordinary people who supported my passion, desire, and vision. It would have been an empty dream without them here to help, guide, and assist me. These people have all listened to me, encouraged me, and allowed me to pursue my passion. First, I must give an enormous thanks to my wonderful wife, Patty. You support my passion, acknowledge my need for accomplishment, and always encourage my love of the sea. I am aware that your love and support are with me every step of the way. Every time I set out to travel up or down the Atlantic coast, your support enables me to leave. Sometimes, days have turned into weeks when I've encountered a problem. I know you have the strength and fortitude to handle it all. You are the most incredible wife a man could have and a wonderful mother to our children. I appreciate all you do to make our family so wonderful! Your love and support mean the world to me. Thank you, Patty, with all my heart.

A big thank-you goes out to my children, Victoria, Jonathan, Julianne, David and Jennifer. You have filled my life in more ways than you will ever know. I know you are busy with college and doing everything young adults need to do. Please follow your dreams and passions, but I also want you to know that I recognize that you allow me to follow my dreams and desires. I am eternally grateful for your support, smiles, laughter, and, most importantly, your love.

My next thank-you goes to Lauri Dorfman, my first mate. Lauri is very competent, skilled, and a capable first mate. Lauri served as my extra set of eyes and has helped me in the acquisition of most of my fleet. Her passion is as strong as my own in life. She has always been ready, able, and willing to do any job needed and was always there for me. I thank her from the bottom of my heart whether she was cleaning filters, reading charts, helping me with docking and anchoring, filling the boat with supplies, driving the boat, or providing some wholesome conversation. With your keen perception and discernment, you helped me face some of the most difficult trips. You are a good friend and a great person. I might add that you are a phenomenal chef who makes everything taste great. Thank you so very much!

Chapter 1
INTRODUCTION

Buying the Right Boat

Buying the right boat is crucial for several reasons, as outlined below:

1. *Safety*: The safety of you, your passengers, and others on the water should be a top priority when purchasing a boat. Different boats are designed for different purposes and water conditions. Buying a boat that is well-suited to your intended use and experience level can enhance safety by reducing the risk of accidents or mishaps.

2. *Comfort and enjoyment*: The right boat will provide you with comfort and enjoyment while on the water. Consider factors such as seating capacity, amenities, and layout to ensure that the boat meets your needs and preferences. Whether you plan to use your boat for fishing, watersports, cruising, or relaxation, choosing a vessel that aligns with your lifestyle will enhance your overall boating experience.

3. *Cost-effectiveness*: Buying the right boat initially can save you money in the long run. Investing in a boat that suits your needs and preferences means you are less likely to incur additional costs for modifications, upgrades, or replacements later on. Additionally, selecting a boat that is fuel-efficient and low-maintenance can help minimize ongoing expenses.

4. *Resale value*: A well-chosen boat is likely to hold its value better over time. Boats that are in high demand within their market segment and well-maintained tend to retain their resale value better than boats that are less popular or poorly maintained. Considering factors such as brand reputation, market demand, and resale history can help you make a more informed decision that maximizes the long-term value of your investment.

5. *Fit for purpose*: Different boats are designed for specific purposes, whether it's fishing, watersports, cruising, or overnight stays. Choosing a boat that is tailored to your intended use ensures that you have the features, capabilities, and performance characteristics necessary to enjoy your favorite activities on the water to the fullest extent.

6. *Ease of ownership*: Owning a boat comes with responsibilities such as maintenance, storage, and insurance. Selecting a boat that is well-suited to your lifestyle and logistical constraints can make ownership more manageable and enjoyable. For example, if you have limited storage space or time for maintenance, opting for a smaller, low-maintenance boat may be more practical than a large, high-maintenance vessel.

In summary, buying the right boat is essential for safety, comfort, cost-effectiveness, resale value, and overall enjoyment of your boating experience. Taking the time to assess your needs, research available options, and make an informed decision will help ensure that you find the perfect boat for your needs and preferences.

Chapter 2
ASSESSING YOUR NEEDS AND BUDGET

Determining Your Boating Goals

Determining your boating goals is an essential first step in the boat-buying process. Your boating goals will influence the type of boat you choose, where you'll use it, and the features and amenities you prioritize. Here's how to effectively determine your boating goals:

1. Identify your purpose.
    - Consider why you want to own a boat. Are you interested in fishing, watersports, cruising, or simply relaxing on the water?
    - Think about the primary activities you envision yourself doing while boating and how frequently you'll engage in them.
2. Assess your experience level.
    - Evaluate your boating experience and skill level. Are you a novice boater looking for a beginner-friendly boat, or do you have years of experience and want a more advanced vessel?
    - Be honest about your comfort level with different types of boats and water conditions.

3. Consider your lifestyle.
   - Reflect on your lifestyle and how a boat fits into it. Are you looking for a weekend getaway, a family-friendly activity, or a way to explore new destinations?
   - Think about how often you'll use the boat and the flexibility you need in terms of scheduling and travel.
4. Evaluate your budget.
   - Determine how much you're willing and able to spend on purchasing and maintaining a boat.
   - Factor in not only the initial purchase price but also ongoing expenses such as insurance, maintenance, fuel, storage, and mooring fees.
5. Research boating locations.
   - Explore the bodies of water near you where you'll likely be boating. Consider factors such as water depth, currents, waves, and any restrictions or regulations that may apply.
   - Determine whether you'll primarily boat on lakes, rivers, coastal waters, or open seas, as different types of boats are better suited to different environments.
6. Consult with others.
   - Seek advice and recommendations from experienced boaters, friends, and family members who own boats.
   - Join boating forums, clubs, or social media groups to connect with other boating enthusiasts and learn from their experiences.
7. Prioritize must-have features.
   - Make a list of the features and amenities that are essential for your boating experience. These may include seating capacity, storage space, onboard facilities (such as a galley or bathroom), and technological advancements (such as navigation systems or entertainment options).
8. Visualize your ideal boat.
   - Take some time to visualize yourself on the water in your ideal boat. Imagine the sights, sounds, and sensa-

tions you'll experience while boating and how the boat you choose will enhance your enjoyment.

By carefully considering these factors and determining your boating goals, you'll be better equipped to select a boat that aligns with your needs, preferences, and lifestyle.

Considering Types of Boats

When considering types of boats to buy, it's essential to evaluate your boating goals, preferences, and intended use. There are various types of boats available, each designed for specific activities and water conditions. Here are some common types of boats to consider:

1. Sailboats:
   - Sailboats are powered primarily by wind, using sails to propel them through the water.
   - They come in various sizes and configurations, including sloops, catamarans, and schooners.
   - Sailboats are ideal for leisurely cruising, racing, and long-distance voyages.
2. Powerboats:
   - Powerboats are motorized vessels that use engines for propulsion.
   - They range from small runabouts and bowriders to larger cruisers, yachts, and motor yachts.
   - Powerboats are versatile and suitable for a wide range of activities, including watersports, fishing, cruising, and day trips.
3. Fishing boats:
   - Fishing boats are designed specifically for angling and typically feature amenities such as fishing rod holders, live wells, and fish finders.
   - They come in various configurations, including center consoles, bass boats, pontoon boats, and offshore fishing boats.

- Fishing boats are equipped to handle different types of fishing, from freshwater bass fishing to offshore deep-sea fishing.

4. Pontoon boats:
   - Pontoon boats have a flat deck supported by pontoons (or tubes) on either side.
   - They are known for their stability, spaciousness, and versatility, making them popular for leisurely cruising, entertaining, and family outings.
   - Pontoon boats often feature comfortable seating, sun loungers, and amenities such as grills, bars, and stereo systems.

5. Personal watercraft (PWC):
   - Personal watercraft, also known as Jet Skis or WaveRunners, are small, agile vessels designed for one to three passengers.
   - They are powered by jet propulsion and offer exhilarating performance for watersports enthusiasts.
   - Personal watercraft are ideal for activities such as riding waves, towing inflatables, and exploring shallow waters.

6. Cabin cruisers:
   - Cabin cruisers are motorized boats with an enclosed cabin for overnight accommodations.
   - They offer amenities such as sleeping quarters, a galley, a bathroom (head), and sometimes even a small salon or entertainment area.
   - Cabin cruisers are suitable for weekend getaways, coastal cruising, and exploring inland waterways.

7. Ski boats / wakeboard boats:
   - Ski boats, also known as wakeboard boats, are designed specifically for watersports such as waterskiing, wakeboarding, and wakesurfing.
   - They feature a specialized hull design, towing pylons or towers, and ballast systems for creating larger wakes.

- Ski boats are equipped with powerful engines and precise handling for towing riders and executing maneuvers.

8. Kayaks and canoes:
    - Kayaks and canoes are paddle-powered vessels designed for solo or tandem use.
    - They are lightweight, portable, and well-suited for exploring narrow waterways, lakes, and calm rivers.
    - Kayaks and canoes are popular for recreational paddling, fishing, and nature watching.

When choosing a boat type, consider factors such as your preferred activities, the number of passengers you'll typically have on board, your experience level, and the water conditions you'll encounter. Additionally, think about storage, transportation, and maintenance requirements to ensure that the boat you select aligns with your needs and lifestyle.

Setting a Realistic Budget

Setting a realistic budget for your first boat is a critical step in the boat-buying process. Here are some steps to help you establish a budget that aligns with your financial situation and boating goals:

1. *Determine your total budget.* Start by evaluating your overall financial situation and determining how much you can comfortably afford to spend on purchasing and owning a boat. Consider factors such as your income, savings, expenses, and existing debt obligations.
2. *Factor in additional costs.* In addition to the purchase price of the boat, consider the various ongoing costs associated with boat ownership. These may include the following:
    - Maintenance and repairs: Budget for routine maintenance tasks such as engine servicing, hull cleaning, and winterization, as well as potential repairs and upgrades.

- Insurance: Obtain quotes for boat insurance coverage to protect your investment against theft, damage, liability, and other risks.
- Mooring or storage fees: If you plan to keep your boat at a marina or storage facility, research the costs of slip rental, dry storage, or trailer storage in your area.
- Registration and licensing: Budget for registration fees, taxes, and any required permits or licenses for operating your boat in your state or country.
- Fuel and operating expenses: Estimate your fuel consumption based on your anticipated usage patterns and the fuel efficiency of the boat you're considering. Also, account for other operating expenses such as docking fees, launch ramp fees, and equipment rentals.
- Additional equipment: Consider the cost of purchasing essential safety equipment, navigation aids, communication devices, and recreational gear for your boat.

3. *Research boat prices.* Research the market prices of boats that meet your criteria in terms of type, size, age, and condition. Use online resources, classified ads, boat listings, and dealership websites to compare prices and get a sense of the price range for boats in your desired category.

4. *Account for financing options.* If you plan to finance your boat purchase, evaluate your borrowing options and calculate the monthly loan payments you can afford. Consider factors such as interest rates, loan terms, down payment requirements, and your creditworthiness.

5. *Be realistic and flexible.* While it's essential to set a budget and stick to it, be prepared to be flexible within your means. Keep in mind that there may be trade-offs between price, features, condition, and age when selecting a boat. Be realistic about what you can afford and prioritize your must-have features while being willing to compromise on less critical aspects if necessary.

6.   *Plan for contingencies.* Build a buffer into your budget to account for unexpected expenses or fluctuations in costs. Having an emergency fund set aside can provide peace of mind and help you manage unforeseen challenges that may arise during the boat-buying process or while owning a boat.

By carefully assessing your financial situation, researching boat prices and ownership costs, and being realistic about your budget constraints, you can set a budget that enables you to find a boat that meets your needs and provides enjoyment on the water without stretching your finances too thin.

Chapter 3
RESEARCHING BOAT TYPES AND FEATURES

Exploring Different Types of Boats (Sailboats, Powerboats, Fishing Boats, etc.)

Exploring different types of boats involves understanding the unique characteristics, uses, and advantages of each type. Here's an overview of some common types of boats:

1. Sailboats:
    - Sailboats are vessels propelled primarily by sails, using the force of the wind to move across the water.
    - They come in various sizes and configurations, from small dinghies and day sailors to large cruising sailboats and racing yachts.
    - Sailboats offer a serene and environmentally friendly way to navigate the water, ideal for leisurely cruising, racing, and long-distance voyages.
    - Key features include masts, sails, rigging, keels or centerboards, and often, auxiliary engines for maneuvering in calm or tight spaces.
2. Powerboats:
    - Powerboats are motorized vessels that use engines for propulsion, offering speed, maneuverability, and convenience.

- They come in a wide range of sizes, styles, and configurations, including runabouts, bowriders, center consoles, cuddy cabins, and motor yachts.
- Powerboats are versatile and suitable for various activities such as watersports, fishing, cruising, day trips, and transportation.
- Key features include hull designs optimized for planing or displacement, outboard or inboard engines, and amenities tailored to specific uses.

3. Fishing boats:
   - Fishing boats are specialized vessels designed for angling, equipped with features and amenities to enhance the fishing experience.
   - They come in various styles, including center consoles, bass boats, pontoon boats, offshore fishing boats, and aluminum johnboats.
   - Fishing boats offer features such as casting decks, fishing rod holders, live wells, fish finders, trolling motors, and storage compartments for gear.
   - They are optimized for different types of fishing, from freshwater bass fishing to offshore deep-sea fishing, and cater to both recreational and professional anglers.

4. Pontoon boats:
   - Pontoon boats feature a flat deck supported by pontoons (or tubes) on either side, offering stability, spaciousness, and versatility.
   - They are popular for leisurely cruising, entertaining, family outings, and watersports such as tubing and waterskiing.
   - Pontoon boats typically offer comfortable seating, sun loungers, tables, and amenities such as grills, bars, stereos, and bimini tops for shade.

5. Personal watercraft (PWC):
   - Personal watercraft, also known as Jet Skis or WaveRunners, are small, agile vessels designed for one to three passengers.

- They are powered by jet propulsion and offer exhilarating performance for activities such as riding waves, towing inflatables, and exploring shallow waters.
- Personal watercraft are popular for recreational use, racing, and watersports, offering speed, maneuverability, and ease of operation.

6. Cabin cruisers:
- Cabin cruisers are motorized boats with an enclosed cabin for overnight accommodations, offering comfort and convenience for extended cruising.
- They feature amenities such as sleeping quarters, a galley, a bathroom (head), and sometimes a small salon or entertainment area.
- Cabin cruisers are suitable for weekend getaways, coastal cruising, and exploring inland waterways, providing a balance of performance, comfort, and livability.

These are just a few examples of the diverse range of boat types available, each offering unique features and advantages to suit different preferences, activities, and water conditions. When exploring different types of boats, consider your boating goals, budget, experience level, and intended use to find the best fit for your needs.

Understanding Boat Features and Options
(Size, Engine Type, Amenities, etc.)

When making a decision about which boat to buy, here's a breakdown of key aspects to consider:

1. Size:
- Boat size impacts its capacity, stability, handling, and comfort.
- Consider the number of passengers you'll typically have onboard and whether you'll need space for gear, equipment, or overnight accommodations.

- Larger boats offer more room for amenities and storage but may be more challenging to maneuver and require larger docking or storage facilities.

2. Engine type:
   - Boat engines vary in type, including outboard, inboard, and sterndrive configurations.
   - Outboard engines are mounted on the transom and provide easy access for maintenance and repairs.
   - Inboard engines are located within the hull, offering better weight distribution and potentially smoother operation.
   - Sterndrive engines combine features of both outboard and inboard engines, with the motor mounted inside the boat and the drive unit located outside.

3. Propulsion system:
   - Propulsion systems determine how the boat moves through the water and affect its performance, fuel efficiency, and handling.
   - Consider factors such as horsepower, torque, fuel consumption, and acceleration when choosing a propulsion system.
   - Common propulsion options include single or multiple outboard motors, inboard engines with shafts or pods, and jet propulsion systems.

4. Amenities:
   - Boat amenities enhance comfort, convenience, and enjoyment while on the water.
   - Common amenities include seating arrangements, sun loungers, dining areas, kitchens (galleys), bathrooms (heads), sleeping quarters, and entertainment systems.
   - Consider your preferences and intended use when evaluating amenities. For example, if you plan to spend long days on the water, comfortable seating and a shaded area may be essential.

5. Hull design:
   - The hull design influences the boat's performance, stability, and seaworthiness.
   - Planing hulls are designed to rise up and ride on the water's surface at high speeds, offering better maneuverability and fuel efficiency.
   - Displacement hulls displace water as they move through it, providing a smoother ride and greater fuel efficiency at lower speeds.
   - Consider the intended use of the boat and the water conditions you'll encounter when choosing a hull design.
6. Navigation and safety equipment:
   - Essential navigation and safety equipment include GPS/chart plotter systems, depth finders, VHF radios, compasses, life jackets, fire extinguishers, and signaling devices.
   - Ensure that the boat is equipped with the necessary safety equipment required by maritime laws and regulations.
7. Customization options:
   - Many boats offer customization options to tailor the vessel to your specific preferences and needs.
   - Explore customization options such as hull colors, upholstery materials, flooring materials, and additional features or accessories.
   - Keep in mind that customization may impact the cost and delivery time of the boat.

Understanding boat features and options allows you to make an informed decision based on your preferences, budget, and intended use. Take the time to research and compare different boats to find the one that best meets your needs and offers the features and amenities you desire.

Assessing New vs. Used Boats

Assessing whether to buy a new or used boat involves considering various factors, including your budget, preferences, and priorities. Here's a comparison to help you make an informed decision:

1. Cost:
   - New boats: New boats typically come with a higher up-front cost due to factors such as depreciation, dealer fees, and taxes. However, they often come with warranties that cover manufacturing defects and provide peace of mind.
   - Used boats: Used boats are generally more affordable up front, as they have already depreciated in value. However, the price can vary depending on factors such as age, condition, and maintenance history. Keep in mind that maintenance and repairs may be required sooner on a used boat.
2. Depreciation:
   - New boats: New boats experience the most significant depreciation in the first few years of ownership. This means that the resale value of a new boat may decrease rapidly during this period.
   - Used boats: Used boats have already undergone initial depreciation, so the rate of depreciation tends to be slower compared to new boats. However, depreciation rates can vary depending on factors such as the boat's age, condition, and market demand.
3. Condition:
   - New boats: New boats are in pristine condition and come with the latest features, technology, and amenities. They also have no wear and tear, making them less likely to require immediate repairs or maintenance.
   - Used boats: The condition of a used boat can vary significantly depending on factors such as age, usage, maintenance history, and previous owners. It's essen-

tial to thoroughly inspect a used boat and consider getting a professional marine survey to assess its condition before purchasing.

4. Customization:
   - New boats: New boats offer the opportunity for customization, allowing you to choose features, amenities, and options to suit your preferences. You can often work with the manufacturer or dealer to customize the boat to your specifications.
   - Used boats: Used boats may already come equipped with features and amenities that may or may not align with your preferences. While some customization options may be available for used boats, they are typically more limited compared to new boats.

5. Availability:
   - New boats: New boats are readily available from manufacturers and dealerships, with a wide selection of models, sizes, and configurations to choose from. However, popular models may have waitlists or limited availability.
   - Used boats: The availability of used boats can vary depending on the market and demand. While there is generally a broader selection of used boats available, finding the right boat in good condition may require more time and effort.

6. Financing and insurance:
   - New boats: Financing options may be more readily available for new boats, with lower interest rates and longer loan terms. Insurance premiums may also be lower for new boats due to their higher resale value and lower risk of mechanical issues.
   - Used boats: Financing for used boats may come with higher interest rates and shorter loan terms. Insurance premiums may also be higher for used boats, depending on factors such as age, condition, and value.

Ultimately, whether to buy a new or used boat depends on your budget, preferences, and priorities. Consider factors such as cost, depreciation, condition, customization options, availability, and financing and insurance considerations when making your decision. Additionally, take the time to thoroughly research and inspect any boat you're considering purchasing to ensure that it meets your needs and expectations.

Chapter 4
UNDERSTANDING
OWNERSHIP COSTS

Initial Purchase Price

Assessing the initial purchase price of your first boat involves several steps to ensure you're getting value for your money and staying within your budget. Here's a guide to help you evaluate the purchase price:

1. Research comparable listings.
   - Start by researching comparable listings for the type, make, model, and year of the boat you're interested in. Look at online marketplaces, classified ads, dealerships, and boat listings to get an idea of the average selling price for similar boats in your area.
2. Consider condition and age.
   - Take into account the age, condition, and overall quality of the boat when assessing its purchase price. Newer boats in excellent condition will generally command higher prices than older boats or those in poor condition.
   - Evaluate factors such as the boat's usage history, maintenance records, any upgrades or modifications, and any signs of wear and tear.

3. Factor in market demand.
   - Consider the current market demand for the type of boat you're interested in. Boats that are in high demand may have higher asking prices, especially during peak boating seasons or in regions with limited availability.
   - Conversely, boats that are less popular or in oversupply may be priced more competitively, offering potential opportunities for savings.
4. Get multiple quotes and estimates.
   - Obtain quotes and estimates from multiple sellers, dealerships, or private sellers to compare prices and negotiate the best deal.
   - Be prepared to haggle and negotiate the purchase price based on factors such as the boat's condition, any necessary repairs or maintenance, and additional features or amenities included in the sale.
5. Consider additional costs.
   - Factor in additional costs associated with purchasing the boat, such as taxes, registration fees, documentation fees, and any optional add-ons or accessories.
   - Keep in mind that there may be ongoing ownership costs to consider, such as insurance, maintenance, storage or mooring fees, fuel, and operating expenses.
6. Evaluate financing options.
   - If you plan to finance your boat purchase, carefully consider the terms and conditions of any loan offers you receive. Compare interest rates, loan terms, down payment requirements, and any associated fees to ensure you're getting the best financing option for your situation.
   - Calculate the total cost of financing over the life of the loan to understand the long-term implications on your budget.
7. Get a professional inspection.
   - Consider hiring a qualified marine surveyor to conduct a thorough inspection of the boat before finalizing

the purchase. A professional inspection can uncover any hidden issues or defects that may affect the boat's value and help you make an informed decision about its purchase price.

8. Set a realistic budget.
   - Finally, set a realistic budget for your boat purchase based on your financial situation, preferences, and priorities. Consider not only the initial purchase price but also any additional costs and ongoing ownership expenses to ensure that you can comfortably afford the boat without overextending yourself financially.

By carefully researching, evaluating, and negotiating the initial purchase price of your first boat, you can make a well-informed decision that aligns with your budget and provides value for your investment.

Maintenance and Repairs

Maintenance and repairs on a boat are essential to ensure its safety, reliability, and longevity. Here's an overview of what maintenance and repairs typically involve:

1. Routine maintenance:
   Regular maintenance tasks are necessary to keep your boat in good condition and prevent potential problems. These tasks may include the following:
   - Cleaning: Regularly clean the hull, deck, interior, and components such as sails, rigging, and engine compartments to remove dirt, salt, and debris.
   - Inspections: Conduct routine inspections of the hull, engine, electrical systems, plumbing, and safety equipment to identify any signs of wear, damage, or corrosion.
   - Lubrication: Apply lubricants to moving parts such as hinges, cleats, winches, and steering

mechanisms to reduce friction and prevent corrosion.

- Fluid checks: Check fluid levels in the engine, transmission, steering, and hydraulic systems, topping up as needed with the appropriate fluids.
- Battery maintenance: Monitor battery condition and charge levels, clean terminals, and perform regular battery checks and maintenance to ensure reliable starting and operation.

2. Engine maintenance:

The boat's engine requires regular maintenance to ensure proper performance and reliability. Tasks may include these:

- Engine checks: Inspect the engine for signs of leaks, corrosion, or damage, and check components such as belts, hoses, filters, and spark plugs.
- Oil changes: Regularly change the engine oil and oil filter according to the manufacturer's recommendations to maintain proper lubrication and engine health.
- Cooling system maintenance: Check and maintain the engine's cooling system, including hoses, water pumps, impellers, and coolant levels, to prevent overheating and corrosion.
- Fuel system maintenance: Inspect the fuel system for leaks, clogs, or contamination, and clean or replace filters, injectors, and fuel lines as needed to ensure proper fuel delivery and combustion.

3. Hull and bottom maintenance:

The boat's hull and bottom require maintenance to prevent fouling, corrosion, and damage. Tasks may include these:

- Bottom cleaning: Regularly clean and inspect the hull bottom to remove marine growth, algae, barnacles, and other fouling organisms that can reduce performance and fuel efficiency.

- Hull inspections: Periodically inspect the hull for signs of damage, blisters, cracks, or delamination, and address any issues promptly to prevent further deterioration.
- Antifouling treatment: Apply antifouling paint or coatings to the hull bottom to inhibit marine growth and protect against corrosion, extending the life span of the hull and improving performance.

4. Electrical and electronics maintenance:

Electrical and electronic systems on the boat require maintenance to ensure proper function and reliability. Tasks may include these:

- Wiring inspections: Inspect electrical wiring, connections, and components for signs of wear, corrosion, or damage, and repair or replace as needed to prevent electrical issues.
- Electronics checks: Test and calibrate navigation equipment, communication devices, GPS systems, depth finders, and other electronics regularly to ensure accurate operation and reliability.
- Battery care: Maintain and monitor batteries, chargers, and charging systems to ensure proper voltage, capacity, and charging cycles, and replace batteries as needed to prevent power failures.

5. Safety equipment maintenance:

Safety equipment on the boat requires regular inspection and maintenance to ensure it functions correctly in case of emergency. Tasks may include these:

- Life rafts and jackets: Inspect and service life rafts, life jackets, and personal flotation devices (PFDs) according to manufacturer guidelines to ensure they are in good condition and properly inflated.
- Fire extinguishers: Check fire extinguishers for proper pressure, condition, and expiration dates,

and recharge or replace them as needed to maintain fire safety onboard.

- Emergency signaling devices: Test and replace batteries in emergency signaling devices such as flares, smoke signals, and distress beacons, and ensure they are readily accessible in case of emergency.

6. Winterization and seasonal maintenance:

Proper winterization and seasonal maintenance are essential to protect the boat during periods of storage or inactivity. Tasks may include these:

- Winterization: Prepare the boat for winter storage by draining water systems, stabilizing fuel, fogging the engine, and protecting vulnerable components from freezing temperatures.
- Seasonal checks: Perform seasonal checks and maintenance tasks before launching the boat each year, including inspections, lubrication, fluid checks, and system tests to ensure readiness for use.

7. Repairs and upgrades:

In addition to routine maintenance, boats may require repairs or upgrades to address wear and tear, damage, or outdated components. Common repairs and upgrades may include these:

- Hull and structural repairs: Addressing damage, cracks, delamination, or blistering in the hull or structural components through patching, filling, fiberglass repairs, or other methods.
- Engine repairs and overhauls: Repairing or replacing engine components, systems, or accessories such as alternators, starters, pumps, or exhaust systems to restore proper function and performance.
- Electrical system repairs: Troubleshooting and repairing electrical issues such as shorts, faults, or

malfunctions in wiring, switches, panels, or electronic devices.
- Cosmetic and aesthetic upgrades: Enhancing the appearance and comfort of the boat through cosmetic upgrades such as new upholstery, flooring, paint, decals, or accessories.

Overall, maintenance and repairs on a boat require regular attention, care, and diligence to ensure the vessel remains safe, reliable, and enjoyable to use. By following a comprehensive maintenance schedule, addressing issues promptly, and investing in quality repairs and upgrades, you can prolong the life of your boat and maximize your enjoyment on the water.

Mooring or Storage Fees

Mooring or storage fees are costs associated with keeping your boat safely secured when it's not in use. These fees can vary depending on the type of storage facility or mooring location you choose and the size of your boat. Here are common types of mooring or storage options and the associated fees:

1. Marina mooring:
   - Marina mooring involves docking your boat at a marina, where it's kept in a designated slip or berth.
   - Marina fees can vary widely depending on factors such as location, amenities, facilities, and the size of the slip.
   - Monthly or annual slip rental fees typically range from a few hundred to several thousand dollars, with additional charges for utilities, amenities (such as electricity and water hookups), and services (such as pump-out, Wi-Fi, and laundry facilities).

2. Dry storage:
    - Dry storage, also known as rack storage or dry stacking, involves storing your boat on land in a covered or uncovered storage facility.
    - Dry storage fees are usually charged on a monthly or annual basis and can vary based on factors such as location, facility amenities, boat size, and storage duration.
    - Monthly dry storage fees typically range from a few hundred to over a thousand dollars, with additional charges for services such as launching, hauling, and winterization.

3. Boatyard storage:
    - Boatyard storage involves storing your boat on land in a boatyard or boat storage facility.
    - Boatyard storage fees may be similar to dry storage fees and can vary depending on factors such as location, amenities, and services offered.
    - Some boatyards offer do-it-yourself (DIY) storage options where boat owners can perform maintenance and repairs on their boats themselves, while others offer full-service options with professional staff available to assist with maintenance and repairs.

4. Trailer storage:
    - Trailer storage involves storing your boat on a trailer when it's not in use, either at your home, a storage facility, or a designated trailer storage yard.
    - Trailer storage fees may be lower than marina or dry storage fees but can vary depending on factors such as location, security, and amenities.
    - Some boat owners choose to store their boats on trailers to save money on storage fees and have the flexibility to transport their boats to different locations for launching and use.

5. Mooring buoy or anchor:
    - Mooring buoys or anchors provide an alternative to docking at a marina by allowing you to secure your boat in a designated mooring field or anchorage area.
    - Mooring fees for buoys or anchorages may be lower than marina fees but can still vary depending on factors such as location, accessibility, and amenities.
    - Some mooring fields may require permits or reservations, and fees may be charged on a daily, weekly, monthly, or seasonal basis.

When budgeting for mooring or storage fees, consider factors such as location, convenience, security, amenities, and your boating habits and preferences. Shop around, compare prices, and consider the overall value and benefits of each mooring or storage option to find the best fit for your needs and budget. Additionally, factor in any additional costs such as transportation, maintenance, insurance, and taxes when calculating the total cost of boat ownership.

Insurance and Registration Costs

Insurance and registration costs for a boat can vary depending on factors such as the type and size of the boat, its value, your location, usage, and insurance coverage options. Here's an overview of the types of insurance and registration costs you may encounter:

1. Boat insurance:
    Boat insurance provides coverage for your boat in the event of damage, theft, liability, and other risks. It's essential to protect your investment and financial well-being.
    Types of boat insurance coverage may include the following:

    a. Hull insurance: Covers physical damage to your boat, including collisions, fire, theft, vandalism, and weather-related incidents.

    b. Liability insurance: Covers bodily injury and property damage liability arising from accidents or incidents involving your boat, including injuries to passengers or damage to other boats or property.

    c. Medical payments coverage: Covers medical expenses for you and your passengers in the event of injuries sustained while on your boat.

    d. Uninsured/underinsured boater coverage: Covers damages and injuries caused by uninsured or underinsured boaters.

    e. Personal effects coverage: Covers personal belongings, equipment, and accessories on your boat, such as electronics, fishing gear, and personal effects.

- Boat insurance premiums can vary based on factors such as the boat's value, age, size, type, usage, navigation area, storage location, safety features, and your insurance history.
- You can obtain boat insurance from specialty marine insurers, as well as from mainstream insurance companies that offer boat insurance as part of their offerings.
- Premiums may be paid annually, semi-annually, or monthly, and discounts may be available for factors such as boating safety courses, safety equipment, and multipolicy bundling.

2. Boat registration and titling:
   - Boat registration and titling requirements vary by state or country and depend on factors such as the boat's size, type, propulsion, and usage.
   - Registration typically involves registering your boat with the appropriate state or federal agency and obtaining registration numbers and validation decals to display on your boat.

- Titling is the process of establishing legal ownership of the boat and receiving a title document similar to a car title.
- Registration and titling fees vary by jurisdiction and may be based on factors such as the boat's length, horsepower, and registration duration.
- In some cases, boats may be exempt from registration or titling requirements, such as certain small boats, nonmotorized boats, or boats used exclusively on private waterways.
- Failure to register or title your boat properly may result in fines, penalties, or restrictions on boating activities.

3. Additional costs:

In addition to insurance and registration costs, there may be other fees and expenses associated with owning a boat:

- Taxes: Some states or jurisdictions may impose sales tax, use tax, or property tax on boat purchases, registrations, or storage.
- Documentation fees: If you choose to document your boat with the US Coast Guard or other authorities, there may be documentation fees associated with the process.
- Inspection fees: Some states or jurisdictions require safety inspections or environmental inspections for certain types of boats or boating activities.
- Renewal fees: Registration, titling, and insurance policies may need to be renewed periodically, with associated renewal fees.

When budgeting for insurance and registration costs for your boat, it's essential to research and understand the requirements and fees specific to your location and circumstances. Shop around for insurance quotes, compare coverage options, and consult with local authorities or insurance agents to ensure that you have the appropriate coverage and meet all legal requirements for owning and operating your boat.

Fuel and Other Operating Expenses

Fuel and other operating expenses for a boat can vary widely depending on factors such as the type of boat, its size, propulsion system, usage patterns, fuel efficiency, maintenance needs, and operating conditions. Here's an overview of the main operating expenses you may encounter:

1. Fuel costs:
   - Fuel costs are a significant operating expense for boat owners, especially for boats with motorized propulsion systems.
   - The amount of fuel consumed depends on factors such as the boat's size, engine type (inboard, outboard, stern drive), horsepower, cruising speed, and fuel efficiency.
   - Fuel prices can fluctuate based on factors such as global oil prices, regional supply and demand, and seasonal variations.
   - Estimating fuel costs involves calculating fuel consumption rates (in gallons per hour or gallons per mile) based on the boat's specifications and usage patterns and multiplying by current fuel prices.
   - Fuel costs can vary significantly depending on how often you use the boat, how far you travel, and the types of activities you engage in (e.g., cruising, fishing, watersports).

2. Maintenance and repairs:
   - Maintenance and repair costs are necessary to keep your boat in good condition and ensure its safety, reliability, and longevity.

- Maintenance tasks may include engine servicing, hull cleaning, bottom painting, propeller maintenance, electrical system checks, and routine inspections.
- Repair costs may arise from unexpected breakdowns, wear and tear, accidents, or damage from environmental factors such as storms or corrosion.
- Budgeting for maintenance and repair costs involves setting aside funds for routine maintenance tasks, as well as establishing an emergency fund to cover unexpected repairs or replacements.

3. Docking and mooring fees:
   - Docking and mooring fees are charges associated with keeping your boat at a marina, yacht club, or other docking facility.
   - Fees may be charged on a monthly, seasonal, or annual basis and can vary depending on factors such as location, amenities, slip size, and availability.
   - Additional charges may apply for services such as electricity, water hookups, pump-out facilities, Wi-Fi access, and amenities such as showers, restrooms, and laundry facilities.

4. Storage fees:
   - Storage fees are costs associated with storing your boat when it's not in use, such as during the offseason or when not in active use.
   - Storage options may include dry storage facilities, boatyards, trailer storage, or marina storage facilities.
   - Fees for storage can vary depending on factors such as location, type of storage (covered or uncovered), boat size, duration, and amenities offered.

5. Insurance premiums:
   - Boat insurance provides coverage for your boat in the event of damage, theft, liability, and other risks.

- Insurance premiums can vary based on factors such as the boat's value, age, size, type, usage, navigation area, storage location, safety features, and your insurance history.
- Premiums may be paid annually, semiannually, or monthly, and discounts may be available for factors such as boating safety courses, safety equipment, and multipolicy bundling.

6. Registration and licensing fees:
   - Registration and licensing fees are charges associated with registering your boat with the appropriate state or federal agency and obtaining the necessary permits or licenses to operate it legally.
   - Fees may be based on factors such as the boat's size, type, propulsion, and registration duration.
   - Failure to register or license your boat properly may result in fines, penalties, or restrictions on boating activities.

7. Other expenses:
   - Other operating expenses may include costs for accessories, equipment, supplies, and recreational gear such as fishing equipment, safety gear, navigation aids, entertainment systems, and onboard amenities.
   - Additional expenses may arise from activities such as boat maintenance courses, safety training, boat rentals or charters, boat club memberships, and travel expenses for boating trips.

When budgeting for fuel and other operating expenses for your boat, it's essential to consider all potential costs and plan accordingly. Keep detailed records of your expenses, monitor your spending, and adjust your budget as needed to ensure that you can afford the ongoing costs of boat ownership while enjoying your boating adventures.

Chapter 5
FINDING THE RIGHT BOAT FOR YOU

Visiting Boat Shows and Dealerships

Visiting boat shows and dealerships can be an excellent way to explore different types of boats and find your first boat. Here's how you can make the most of these opportunities:

1. Research beforehand.
    - Before attending a boat show or dealership visit, research the types of boats available, their features, and their suitability for your needs and preferences.
    - Consider factors such as boat size, type (sailboat, powerboat, fishing boat, etc.), propulsion system, amenities, and budget to narrow down your options.

2. Attend boat shows.
    - Boat shows are events where manufacturers, dealers, and vendors showcase their latest boat models, accessories, and marine products.
    - Attend boat shows in your area or region to see a wide variety of boats from different manufacturers and dealers all in one place.

- Take advantage of the opportunity to board and inspect different boats, ask questions, and compare features, designs, and prices.
- Boat shows often offer special promotions, discounts, and financing options, making it an ideal time to make a purchase or negotiate a deal.

3. Visit dealerships.
   - Visit local boat dealerships to view their inventory of new and used boats and speak with sales representatives.
   - Dealerships typically have a range of boats on display, including various models, sizes, and configurations to suit different preferences and budgets.
   - Take the time to explore different boats, sit in the cockpit or cabin, and imagine yourself onboard to assess comfort, layout, and features.
   - Ask questions about the boats' specifications, performance, maintenance requirements, and available options and request test rides or sea trials to experience how the boats handle on the water.

4. Consult with experts.
   - Take advantage of the expertise and knowledge of sales representatives, boat dealers, and industry professionals at boat shows and dealerships.
   - Seek guidance and advice on choosing the right boat for your needs, budget, and experience level.
   - Ask for recommendations, tips, and insights on boat ownership, maintenance, and safety best practices.

5. Compare options.
   - Take notes and photos of the boats you're interested in and compare their features, prices, and overall value.
   - Consider factors such as build quality, reputation of the manufacturer or brand, resale value, warranty cov-

erage, and after-sales support when evaluating different boats.

- Don't feel pressured to make a decision on the spot. Take your time to weigh your options, gather information, and make an informed decision that aligns with your needs and preferences.

6. Arrange financing.
    - If you plan to finance your boat purchase, explore financing options and preapproval before visiting boat shows or dealerships.
    - Research lenders, loan terms, interest rates, and repayment options to find the best financing solution for your situation.
    - Be prepared to provide financial documentation, such as income verification, credit history, and employment information, when applying for a boat loan.

By attending boat shows and visiting dealerships, you can gain valuable insights, explore different boats up close, and make informed decisions about your first boat purchase. Take your time, ask questions, and enjoy the process of finding the perfect boat to embark on your boating adventures.

Browsing Online Listings and Classifieds

Browsing online listings and classifieds is another excellent way to find your first boat. Here's how to effectively navigate these platforms:

1. Choose reputable websites.
    - Start by visiting reputable websites that specialize in boat sales, such as BoatTrader, YachtWorld, Boats. com, Craigslist, or local classifieds.

- Look for websites with a large inventory of boats, user-friendly search tools, detailed listings, and trusted seller ratings or reviews.

2. Use advanced search filters.
   - Utilize advanced search filters to narrow down your options based on criteria such as boat type, size, price range, location, age, and features.
   - Specify your preferences to refine your search results and focus on boats that meet your specific needs and budget.

3. Review listings carefully.
   - Take your time to review each listing carefully and thoroughly.
   - Look for detailed descriptions, specifications, and photos of the boats to assess their condition, features, and suitability.
   - Pay attention to key details such as boat length, make, model, year, propulsion type, engine hours, amenities, and any included equipment or accessories.

4. Compare prices and value.
   - Compare prices across different listings to get an idea of the market value for similar boats.
   - Consider factors such as boat condition, age, equipment, maintenance history, and included extras when evaluating the overall value of each listing.
   - Be cautious of listings that seem significantly underpriced as they may indicate hidden issues or scams.

5. Contact sellers and ask questions.
   - Reach out to sellers directly through the online platform to ask questions, request additional information, or schedule viewings or inspections.

- Inquire about the boat's history, maintenance records, usage, storage, and any known issues or concerns.
- Request high-resolution photos or videos of specific areas or features if needed to make an informed decision.

6. Arrange viewings and inspections.
   - If possible, arrange to view the boat in person or schedule a professional inspection to assess its condition and functionality.
   - Inspect the boat thoroughly, both inside and out, and test any equipment, systems, or features to ensure they are in good working order.
   - Look for signs of wear, damage, or neglect and ask the seller about any observed issues or discrepancies.

7. Negotiate and complete the purchase.
   - If you find a boat that meets your criteria and budget, negotiate the price and terms with the seller to reach a mutually acceptable agreement.
   - Be prepared to negotiate based on factors such as the boat's condition, market value, comparable listings, and any necessary repairs or upgrades.
   - Once you've agreed on a price, arrange for payment, paperwork, and any necessary documentation to complete the purchase transaction.

8. Ensure legal compliance.
   - Ensure that the boat has a clear title and all necessary documentation for registration, licensing, and ownership transfer.
   - Verify that the seller has the legal authority to sell the boat and that there are no outstanding liens, encumbrances, or legal issues associated with the vessel.

Browsing online listings and classifieds allows you to explore a wide range of boats from the comfort of your home and find options that meet your preferences and budget. By following these tips and conducting thorough research, you can make an informed decision and find the perfect boat for your needs and adventures.

Consulting with Experienced Boaters

Consulting with experienced boaters can provide valuable insights and advice when buying your first boat. Here are some ways and places to find experienced boaters for consultation:

1. Local boating clubs and associations:
   - Joining local boating clubs or associations is an excellent way to connect with experienced boaters in your area.
   - Attend club meetings, events, or social gatherings to network with fellow boaters, share experiences, and seek advice.
   - Many boating clubs also offer educational programs, seminars, or mentorship opportunities for novice boaters to learn from experienced members.

2. Marinas and yacht clubs:
   - Visit marinas and yacht clubs in your area and strike up conversations with boat owners and enthusiasts.
   - Many marinas and yacht clubs have community bulletin boards, social spaces, or organized events where boaters gather and exchange information.
   - Ask for recommendations or referrals to experienced boaters who may be willing to offer guidance or assistance.

3. Online boating forums and communities:
    *   Joining online boating forums, discussion groups, or social media communities can connect you with a diverse network of boaters from around the world.
    *   Participate in discussions, ask questions, and seek advice from experienced members who have firsthand knowledge and insights.
    *   Look for forums or groups dedicated to specific types of boats, boating activities, or regions to find relevant information and resources.

4. Boat shows and events:
    *   Attend boat shows, expos, rendezvous, or other boating events where you can meet and interact with experienced boaters, boat owners, dealers, and industry professionals.
    *   Take advantage of networking opportunities, seminars, workshops, or educational sessions offered at these events to learn from experts and experienced boaters.

5. Boat dealerships and brokers:
    *   Visit local boat dealerships, brokers, or marine retailers and consult with knowledgeable sales representatives or brokers who have experience in the boating industry.
    *   Sales professionals can provide information, guidance, and recommendations based on your preferences, budget, and boating goals.
    *   Ask to speak with experienced boaters or boat owners who may be affiliated with the dealership or brokerage for additional insights.

6. Boat rental or charter companies:
    *   Renting or chartering a boat is an opportunity to interact with experienced captains, crew members, or

instructors who can offer guidance, instruction, and advice.
- Take advantage of instructional charters, guided tours, or boat rental services that provide hands-on experience and personalized instruction for novice boaters.

7. Personal connections and referrals:
- Reach out to friends, family members, colleagues, or acquaintances who are experienced boaters or have connections in the boating community.
- Ask for recommendations or introductions to experienced boaters who may be willing to share their knowledge, offer guidance, or provide mentorship.

When consulting with experienced boaters, be respectful of their time and expertise, and approach them with specific questions or areas where you seek advice or assistance. Be open to learning from their experiences, insights, and recommendations to help you make informed decisions and navigate the process of buying your first boat successfully.

Considering Prepurchase Surveys

A prepurchase survey for a boat is a comprehensive inspection conducted by a qualified marine surveyor to assess the condition, value, and overall seaworthiness of a vessel before purchasing it. Here's what you need to know about prepurchase surveys for your first boat:

1. Purpose:
- The primary purpose of a prepurchase survey is to provide the buyer with a detailed assessment of the boat's condition, identify any existing or potential problems, and determine its value relative to its condition and market factors.

- The survey helps buyers make informed decisions and negotiate fair terms based on the boat's condition and any necessary repairs or upgrades.

2. Scope:
   - A prepurchase survey typically includes a thorough examination of the boat's structure, systems, equipment, and overall condition.
   - The surveyor will inspect the hull, deck, superstructure, rigging (if applicable), propulsion system, electrical system, plumbing, fuel system, safety equipment, and other components.
   - The survey may also include sea trials (on-water tests) to evaluate the boat's performance, handling, and systems under real-world conditions.

3. Surveyor qualifications:
   - It's essential to hire a qualified and accredited marine surveyor with experience and expertise in conducting prepurchase surveys for boats.
   - Look for surveyors who are members of professional organizations such as the Society of Accredited Marine Surveyors (SAMS) or the National Association of Marine Surveyors (NAMS) and have appropriate certifications and credentials.

4. Process:
   - The prepurchase survey process typically begins with scheduling an appointment with the surveyor and coordinating access to the boat for inspection.
   - The surveyor will conduct a thorough examination of the boat, documenting findings, taking measurements, and recording observations.
   - Depending on the boat's size, complexity, and condition, the survey may take several hours or more to complete.

- After the inspection, the surveyor will prepare a detailed written report outlining their findings, observations, recommendations, and any areas of concern.

5. Areas covered:
   During the survey, the surveyor will assess various aspects of the boat including these:
   - Structural integrity: Hull condition, deck condition, bulkheads, stringers, and structural components.
   - Mechanical systems: Engine(s), transmission, propulsion system, steering system, fuel system, cooling system, and exhaust system.
   - Electrical systems: Wiring, switches, panels, batteries, charging systems, lighting, and electronics.
   - Plumbing systems: Freshwater system, wastewater system, pumps, hoses, and fittings.
   - Safety equipment: Life-saving appliances, fire extinguishers, bilge pumps, navigation lights, and signaling devices.
   - Miscellaneous equipment: Anchoring gear, mooring equipment, ventilation systems, and other accessories.

6. Findings and recommendations:
   - The surveyor's report will summarize their findings and recommendations, including any deficiencies, defects, or areas needing attention.
   - Based on the survey findings, the buyer can negotiate with the seller to address identified issues, adjust the purchase price, or determine whether to proceed with the purchase.
   - In some cases, the survey may uncover significant issues that prompt the buyer to reconsider the purchase or seek further evaluation from specialists (e.g.,

engine mechanics, rigging experts, or fiberglass repair technicians).

7. Cost:
    *   The cost of a prepurchase survey varies depending on factors such as the boat's size, type, complexity, location, and the surveyor's rates.
    *   Expect to pay several hundred to several thousand dollars for a comprehensive prepurchase survey, depending on the scope of the inspection and the surveyor's fees.

In summary, a prepurchase survey is a crucial step in the boat-buying process that provides buyers with valuable information and peace of mind when making a significant investment in a boat. By hiring a qualified surveyor and conducting a thorough inspection, buyers can make informed decisions and ensure that they are purchasing a seaworthy and well-maintained vessel.

Chapter 6
INSPECTING AND SEA-TRIALING POTENTIAL BOATS

Conducting a Visual Inspection

Conducting a visual inspection is an essential part of evaluating the condition of a boat before purchase. Here's a step-by-step process for conducting a visual inspection:

1. Exterior inspection:
    - Start by examining the exterior of the boat, including the hull, deck, and superstructure.
    - Look for signs of damage, such as cracks, scratches, dents, or gouges in the gelcoat or fiberglass.
    - Check for evidence of repairs, patches, or mismatched paint or gelcoat that may indicate previous damage or repairs.
    - Inspect the hull for signs of osmotic blistering, delamination, or water intrusion, especially along the waterline and below the waterline.
    - Check the condition of the keel, rudder, and other underwater appendages for damage, corrosion, or signs of grounding.

- Look for stress cracks or crazing around fittings, through-hull openings, and areas of high stress or flex.

2. Structural inspection:
   - Assess the structural integrity of the boat by examining bulkheads, stringers, and other internal components.
   - Look for signs of rot, decay, or water damage in wooden components such as bulkheads, stringers, and cabinetry.
   - Tap on fiberglass components with a rubber mallet to listen for delamination or voids, which may produce a hollow sound.
   - Inspect the transom for signs of rot, delamination, or separation, especially around through-hull fittings and mounting points for engines or accessories.

3. Deck inspection:
   - Check the deck for soft spots, flexing, or delamination, which may indicate water intrusion or structural damage.
   - Inspect the integrity of deck hardware, including cleats, stanchions, railings, and lifelines, and ensure they are securely fastened and free of corrosion or damage.
   - Look for cracks or crazing in nonskid surfaces, as well as signs of wear or deterioration in deck coatings or sealants.

4. Hardware and fittings:
   - Examine all hardware, fittings, and accessories on the boat for signs of wear, corrosion, or damage.
   - Check cleats, winches, tracks, blocks, and other hardware for proper operation and secure attachment.
   - Inspect through-hull fittings, sea cocks, and valves for leaks, corrosion, or signs of deterioration, and ensure they operate smoothly.

5. Rigging and mast inspection (for sailboats):
    - If the boat is a sailboat, inspect the rigging, mast, and sails for wear, damage, or signs of fatigue.
    - Check the condition of standing rigging (shrouds and stays), running rigging (halyards and sheets), and sail controls (furlers, reefing systems, etc.).
    - Look for broken strands, kinks, rust, or signs of fatigue in wire rigging and check swage fittings, turnbuckles, and tangs for corrosion or damage.

6. Engine and mechanical systems:
    - Inspect the engine(s), propulsion system, and mechanical components for signs of wear, leaks, or damage.
    - Check fluid levels, hoses, belts, filters, and other engine components for proper operation and condition.
    - Run the engine(s) to check for smooth operation, proper starting, and any unusual noises, vibrations, or smoke.
    - Inspect fuel tanks, lines, and filters for leaks, corrosion, or contamination and check the condition of the exhaust system.

7. Electrical systems:
    - Evaluate the condition of the boat's electrical systems, including wiring, switches, panels, and accessories.
    - Check for loose connections, corroded terminals, or damaged wiring and ensure electrical components are properly secured and protected from moisture.
    - Test lighting, navigation lights, instrumentation, electronics, and other electrical devices for proper operation.

8. Interior inspection:
    - Finally, inspect the interior of the boat, including the cabin, cockpit, and living spaces.

- Look for signs of water intrusion, leaks, or mildew in upholstery, cushions, headliners, and cabinetry.
- Check for proper operation of doors, hatches, windows, and ventilation systems and ensure they are watertight and secure.

By following this visual inspection process, you can identify potential issues, assess the overall condition of the boat, and make an informed decision about its suitability for purchase. If you're unsure about any aspect of the inspection or need assistance, consider hiring a qualified marine surveyor to conduct a more comprehensive evaluation of the boat.

Assessing Structural Integrity

Assessing the structural integrity of a boat is crucial to ensure its seaworthiness and safety. Here's how you can assess the structural integrity of a boat:

1. Visual inspection:
   - Begin by visually inspecting the boat's hull, deck, and superstructure for any visible signs of damage, such as cracks, dents, scratches, or blisters.
   - Look for areas where the gelcoat or fiberglass may be compromised, indicating potential structural issues.
   - Check for any signs of previous repairs or modifications, and assess their quality and effectiveness.

2. Tap test:
   - Use a small mallet or hammer to gently tap along the hull, deck, and other structural components.
   - Listen for any hollow or dull sounds, which could indicate delamination or voids in the fiberglass laminate.
   - Solid uniform sounds typically indicate a sound structure while hollow or dull sounds may indicate areas of concern.

3. Compression test:
    *   Apply pressure to different areas of the deck and hull using your hands or by standing on various sections.
    *   Pay attention to any areas that feel soft, flex excessively, or give under pressure as these may indicate delamination, rot, or structural weakness.
    *   Soft spots or flexing in the deck or hull may suggest underlying structural issues that require further investigation.

4. Moisture meter:
    *   Use a moisture meter to assess the moisture content of the fiberglass laminate.
    *   Check for elevated moisture levels, especially in areas prone to water intrusion, such as around through-hull fittings, hardware penetrations, or areas of impact or damage.
    *   High moisture levels may indicate delamination, rot, or water intrusion into the laminate, which can compromise the structural integrity of the boat.

5. Professional survey:
    *   Consider hiring a qualified marine surveyor to conduct a comprehensive inspection of the boat's structural integrity.
    *   A marine surveyor will have the expertise, experience, and specialized equipment necessary to assess the boat's structural condition thoroughly.
    *   The surveyor will inspect the hull, deck, and other structural components, conduct moisture readings, and provide a detailed report outlining any issues or recommendations.

6. Sea trial:
    *   Conduct a sea trial to assess the boat's handling, stability, and structural integrity under real-world conditions.

- Pay attention to any unusual vibrations, noises, or handling characteristics that may indicate structural issues or deficiencies.
- Test the boat's performance in various sea states and maneuvers to evaluate its stability and seaworthiness.

7. Manufacturer documentation:
   - Review the boat's manufacturer documentation, including construction plans, specifications, and maintenance guidelines.
   - Check for any known structural issues, recalls, or recommended inspection and maintenance procedures outlined by the manufacturer.
   - Consult with knowledgeable professionals, such as boatbuilders, designers, or engineers, for additional insights into the boat's structural integrity.

By following these steps and conducting a thorough assessment of the boat's structural integrity, you can identify any potential issues or concerns and make an informed decision about its suitability for purchase. If you're unsure about any aspect of the inspection or need assistance, consider consulting with experienced professionals, such as marine surveyors or boatbuilders, for expert guidance and advice.

Checking Mechanical Systems

Checking the mechanical systems of a boat is essential to ensure its reliability, performance, and safety on the water. Here's how you can conduct a thorough inspection of the boat's mechanical systems:

1. Engine and propulsion system:
   - Start by inspecting the engine(s), transmission, and propulsion system for signs of wear, damage, or corrosion.

- Check fluid levels, including engine oil, coolant, hydraulic fluid, and gear lubricant, and look for any signs of leaks or contamination.
- Inspect hoses, belts, and fittings for cracks, deterioration, or leaks and replace any worn or damaged components as needed.
- Verify proper operation of engine controls, throttle, shifters, and steering systems and ensure they respond smoothly and accurately.
- Run the engine(s) to check for smooth starting, idling, acceleration, and operation underload and listen for any unusual noises, vibrations, or exhaust smoke.
- Test the operation of the propulsion system, including propeller(s), shaft(s), and drive unit(s), and ensure they are properly aligned and free of damage or fouling.

2. Electrical systems:
   - Evaluate the boat's electrical systems, including wiring, switches, panels, and accessories.
   - Check for loose connections, corroded terminals, or damaged wiring and ensure electrical components are properly secured and protected from moisture.
   - Test lighting, navigation lights, instrument panel gauges, electronics, and other electrical devices for proper operation.
   - Inspect the battery(s), charging system, and voltage regulator for signs of corrosion, damage, or malfunction and ensure they are functioning correctly.
   - Test safety features such as bilge pumps, horn, and emergency lighting to ensure they operate as intended.

3. Fuel system:
   - Inspect the fuel system components, including fuel tanks, hoses, filters, and fittings, for signs of leaks, corrosion, or deterioration.

- Check fuel lines and connections for tightness and security and replace any worn or damaged components as needed.
- Test fuel system components such as fuel pumps, filters, and fuel/water separators for proper operation and flow.
- Inspect fuel tank(s) for signs of corrosion, leaks, or contamination and ensure they are properly secured and vented.

4. Cooling system:
   - Assess the boat's cooling system, including raw water and freshwater cooling systems for engine(s) and other components.
   - Check for leaks, corrosion, or blockages in cooling system hoses, fittings, and heat exchangers and replace any worn or damaged components.
   - Verify proper circulation and temperature control in the cooling system and monitor engine temperature gauges during operation.
   - Inspect raw water intake and discharge fittings, strainers, and sea chests for blockages or fouling and clean or replace components as needed.

5. Exhaust system:
   - Inspect the boat's exhaust system, including exhaust manifolds, risers, elbows, mufflers, and through-hull fittings.
   - Check for leaks, corrosion, or damage in exhaust system components and ensure they are properly secured and vented.
   - Monitor exhaust gas temperatures and check for proper exhaust gas flow during engine operation.

6. Steering and controls:
   - Check the boat's steering system, including cables, hydraulic lines, and mechanical linkages for proper operation and alignment.
   - Test the responsiveness and accuracy of steering controls, including wheel, tiller, or joystick steering systems.
   - Verify proper operation of throttle, shifters, trim controls, and other engine controls and ensure they respond smoothly and accurately.

7. Safety devices and emergency equipment:
   - Test safety devices such as bilge pumps, fire extinguishers, and emergency shutoff switches to ensure they operate as intended.
   - Verify the presence and condition of safety equipment such as life jackets, flares, distress signals, and emergency medical supplies.

By following these steps and conducting a thorough inspection of the boat's mechanical systems, you can identify any potential issues or concerns and ensure that the boat is in good working order before purchase. If you're unsure about any aspect of the inspection or need assistance, consider consulting with experienced marine mechanics or technicians for expert guidance and advice.

Test-Driving the Boat

Yes, conducting a test drive, also known as a sea trial, is highly recommended when buying a boat. Here's why it's important and how to go about it:

1. Assess performance. A sea trial allows you to evaluate the boat's performance and handling characteristics in real-world conditions. This includes testing its acceleration,

maneuverability, turning radius, stability, and overall responsiveness.

2. Check mechanical systems. During the sea trial, you can assess the operation of the boat's mechanical systems, including the engine(s), propulsion system, steering, and controls. This allows you to identify any issues or abnormalities, such as unusual noises, vibrations, or performance issues, that may not be apparent during a static inspection.

3. Evaluate comfort and ergonomics. Testing the boat on the water allows you to experience its comfort and ergonomics firsthand. This includes assessing factors such as seating arrangements, visibility from the helm, noise levels, and ride quality. You can determine whether the boat meets your comfort and usability preferences, especially during extended periods on the water.

4. Check for leaks or water intrusion. A sea trial provides an opportunity to check for leaks or water intrusion into the hull, deck, or other areas of the boat. You can observe whether the bilge pumps operate as intended and monitor for any signs of water ingress, such as water pooling in the bilge or cabin.

5. Confirm safety equipment. During the sea trial, you can verify the functionality of safety equipment such as navigation lights, horn, and other signaling devices. You can also assess the effectiveness of safety features such as handrails, grab handles, and nonskid surfaces in various conditions.

6. Confirm boat's condition. A sea trial allows you to confirm the overall condition of the boat and verify that it meets your expectations and requirements. It provides an opportunity to address any concerns or questions that may arise

during the test drive and make an informed decision about the purchase.

To conduct a sea trial, do the following:
- Schedule the sea trial with the seller or dealer at a mutually convenient time and location.
- Bring along any necessary safety equipment, such as life jackets, as well as a checklist of items to inspect and test during the sea trial.
- Before setting out, discuss with the seller or dealer the specific areas you'd like to test or evaluate during the sea trial.

During the sea trial, take note of any observations, concerns, or questions that arise and communicate them to the seller or dealer for further discussion.

After the sea trial, review your notes and observations and use this information to inform your decision-making process when considering the purchase of the boat.

Overall, conducting a sea trial is a crucial step in the boat-buying process as it provides valuable insights into the boat's performance, condition, and suitability for your needs and preferences.

Chapter 7
NEGOTIATING THE PURCHASE

Understanding Negotiation Strategies

Negotiating the purchase of a boat can be a complex process, but having a solid understanding of negotiation strategies can help you secure a fair deal. Here are some key strategies to consider when buying a boat:

1. Do your research.

    Before entering negotiations, research the market value of similar boats in terms of make, model, age, condition, and features. This information will give you a baseline for determining a fair price and will strengthen your negotiating position.

2. Set your budget.

    Determine your budget and establish the maximum amount you're willing to pay for the boat. Consider not only the purchase price but also additional costs such as taxes, registration, insurance, and maintenance.

3. Identify your priorities.

    Understand your priorities and preferences regarding the boat's features, condition, and equipment. Identify any must-have features as well as areas where you're willing to compromise.

4. Be prepared to walk away.

    One of the most powerful negotiation tactics is being willing to walk away from the deal if it doesn't meet your criteria or budget. This demonstrates to the seller that you're serious and not willing to settle for a subpar offer.

5. Start with a reasonable offer.

    Begin negotiations with a reasonable but slightly lower offer than your maximum budget. This allows room for negotiation while still showing the seller that you're serious about making a purchase.

6. Highlight value.

    Emphasize the value of your offer by highlighting any unique features, recent upgrades, or improvements that the boat may have. Show the seller why your offer is fair and reasonable given the boat's condition and market value.

7. Negotiate incrementally:

    Use incremental negotiation tactics by making small concessions or adjustments to your offer while seeking reciprocal concessions from the seller. This gradual approach can help bridge the gap between your initial offer and the seller's asking price.

8. Focus on win-win solutions.

    Approach negotiations with a collaborative mindset and seek win-win solutions that benefit both parties. Look for areas where you can add value or offer incentives to sweeten the deal, such as agreeing to a quick closing or covering certain closing costs.

9. Be respectful and professional.

    Maintain a respectful and professional demeanor throughout the negotiation process, even if discussions become tense or challenging. Avoid making personal attacks or aggressive demands as this can derail negotiations and sour the relationship with the seller.

10. Get everything in writing.

    Once you've reached an agreement, make sure to get all terms and conditions in writing, including the purchase

price, any included equipment or accessories, financing terms, and timelines for inspection, closing, and delivery.
11. Consider using a broker.

If you're uncomfortable negotiating directly with the seller or need assistance navigating the process, consider hiring a professional boat broker or agent. A skilled broker can represent your interests, provide expert advice, and handle negotiations on your behalf.

By employing these negotiation strategies and tactics, you can increase your chances of securing a favorable deal when buying a boat while also fostering a positive and mutually beneficial relationship with the seller.

Making a Reasonable Offer

Making a reasonable offer when buying a boat is essential for initiating negotiations and securing a fair deal. Here's how the process typically works:

1. Research market value.

Before making an offer, research the market value of similar boats. Consider factors such as the make, model, year, condition, equipment, and location. Use online resources, boat valuation guides, and sales listings to gather information on comparable boats.
2. Evaluate the boat's condition.

Assess the condition of the boat you're interested in purchasing. Consider factors such as its overall condition, maintenance history, upgrades, and any deficiencies or areas needing attention. Take note of any features or improvements that add value to the boat.
3. Determine your budget.

Establish your budget and determine the maximum amount you're willing to pay for the boat. Consider additional costs such as taxes, registration, insurance, and any necessary repairs or upgrades. Be realistic about what you can afford and factor in future expenses for ownership and maintenance.

4. Consider market conditions.

   Take into account current market conditions and trends when making your offer. In a buyer's market where inventory is high and demand is low, you may have more negotiating leverage. Conversely, in a seller's market where demand exceeds supply, sellers may be less inclined to accept lower offers.

5. Start with a reasonable offer.

   Begin negotiations by making a reasonable but slightly lower offer than your maximum budget. This provides room for negotiation while still demonstrating your seriousness as a buyer. Avoid making lowball offers that may offend the seller and hinder further negotiations.

6. Support your offer.

   Support your offer by providing rationale or justification based on the boat's market value, condition, and comparable sales. Highlight any unique features, recent upgrades, or improvements that add value to the boat. Present your offer in a respectful and professional manner and be prepared to explain your reasoning to the seller.

7. Be prepared to negotiate.

   Expect the seller to respond to your offer with a counteroffer or additional terms. Be prepared to engage in negotiations and consider potential compromises or adjustments to reach a mutually acceptable agreement. Remain flexible and open-minded throughout the negotiation process.

8. Evaluate counteroffers.

   Evaluate any counteroffers or responses from the seller carefully. Consider the seller's position, their reasons for rejecting or modifying your offer, and whether the proposed terms align with your priorities and budget. Assess whether the counteroffer represents fair value based on market conditions and the boat's condition.

9. Finalize terms and conditions.

Once you and the seller have reached an agreement on the purchase price and terms, ensure that all details are clearly documented in writing. Review and finalize the terms and conditions of the sale, including any contingencies, deadlines, or conditions of sale. Be prepared to provide a deposit or earnest money to secure the agreement.

10. Proceed with due diligence.

After reaching an agreement, proceed with due diligence by conducting inspections, surveys, and any necessary evaluations to confirm the boat's condition and address any contingencies or concerns. Work closely with the seller to coordinate inspections and finalize the sale transaction.

By following these steps and making a reasonable offer based on market research, the boat's condition, and your budget, you can initiate negotiations with confidence and increase your chances of securing a favorable deal when buying a boat.

Addressing Inspection Findings

Addressing inspection findings typically involves a structured approach to ensure that all identified issues are acknowledged, properly investigated, and effectively resolved. Here's a general guideline on how to address inspection findings:

1. *Review findings thoroughly.* Carefully read through the inspection report to understand each finding in detail. Ensure you comprehend the nature and severity of each issue.

2. *Prioritize findings.* Classify findings based on their level of criticality and potential impact. This helps in determining which issues need immediate attention versus those that can be addressed over time.

3. *Identify root causes.* Conduct further investigation, if necessary, to determine the root causes of the identified issues. Understanding why problems occurred is crucial for implementing effective corrective actions.

4. *Develop a corrective action plan.* Formulate a detailed plan outlining specific actions to be taken to address each finding. Assign responsibilities to relevant individuals or teams for implementing corrective actions.

5. *Set clear deadlines.* Establish realistic timelines for addressing each finding. Ensure deadlines are feasible and allow sufficient time for thorough resolution.

6. *Implement corrective actions.* Execute the planned corrective actions according to the established timeline. Monitor progress closely to ensure actions are being carried out effectively.

7. *Communicate progress.* Keep stakeholders informed about the progress of corrective actions. Provide regular updates on the status of each finding and any challenges encountered during the resolution process.

8. *Verify effectiveness.* Once corrective actions have been implemented, verify their effectiveness by conducting follow-up inspections or audits. Ensure that the identified issues have been adequately resolved and that similar problems are less likely to recur.

9. *Document everything.* Maintain detailed records of all actions taken to address inspection findings. This documentation serves as evidence of compliance and can be valuable for future reference or audits.

10. *Continuous improvement.* Use the findings and lessons learned from the inspection process to improve existing processes, procedures, and systems. Implement measures to prevent similar issues from arising in the future. By fol-

lowing these steps, you can effectively address inspection findings and ensure that your organization maintains compliance, quality, and safety standards.

Finalizing the Deal

Finalizing a deal involves several crucial steps to ensure that all parties involved are satisfied with the terms and conditions and that the agreement is legally binding. Here's a comprehensive guide on how to finalize a deal:

1. Negotiation: Prior to finalizing a deal, negotiations take place where both parties discuss and agree on the terms, conditions, and specifics of the agreement. This involves thorough discussion, compromise, and reaching a mutually beneficial arrangement.
2. Drafting the agreement: Once the negotiations are complete, a formal agreement outlining the terms of the deal is drafted. This document should clearly specify the rights, obligations, and responsibilities of each party involved.
3. Review by legal counsel: It's essential for both parties to have the agreement reviewed by their respective legal counsel to ensure that it complies with relevant laws and regulations and adequately protects their interests.
4. Due diligence: Depending on the nature of the deal, due diligence may be conducted to verify the accuracy of the information provided and assess any potential risks associated with the agreement.
5. Signing the agreement: Once all parties are satisfied with the terms and conditions outlined in the agreement, they proceed to sign it. This can be done in person, electronically, or through authorized representatives.
6. Execution of conditions precedent: Some agreements may have conditions precedent that need to be fulfilled before the deal can be finalized. These conditions could include

obtaining regulatory approvals, securing financing, or completing certain actions.

7. Exchange of consideration: In many deals, there is an exchange of consideration, such as payment or assets, between the parties involved. This exchange typically occurs at the time of signing the agreement or upon fulfillment of specific conditions.

8. Sealing the deal: Once all the necessary steps have been completed, the deal is considered finalized. Both parties are bound by the terms and conditions outlined in the agreement, and they are expected to fulfill their respective obligations.

9. Recordkeeping: It's important to maintain accurate records of the finalized deal, including the signed agreement and any relevant documentation. These records serve as proof of the agreement and can be referred to in the event of disputes or disagreements in the future.

10. Postclosing activities: After the deal is finalized, there may be additional tasks to be completed, such as transferring ownership of assets, integrating operations, or fulfilling any postclosing obligations specified in the agreement.

By following these steps, you can ensure that the deal is finalized smoothly and effectively, minimizing the risk of misunderstandings or disputes and laying the groundwork for a successful business relationship.

Chapter 8

COMPLETING THE PURCHASE

Securing Financing (if Applicable)

Securing financing is a critical step in finalizing many types of deals, especially those involving significant financial transactions such as mergers and acquisitions, real estate purchases, or large-scale business expansions. Here's a guide on how to secure financing as part of the deal finalization process:

1. *Assess financing needs.* Determine the amount of financing required to complete the deal. This involves evaluating the total cost of the transaction, including purchase price, fees, taxes, and other expenses.

2. *Explore financing options.* Research and evaluate various financing options available based on the specific needs and circumstances of the deal. Common sources of financing include bank loans, venture capital, private equity, asset-based lending, crowdfunding, and government grants or loans.

3. *Prepare financial documentation.* Compile all necessary financial documentation required by potential lenders or investors. This typically includes financial statements, business plans, cash flow projections, collateral information, and any other relevant financial data.

4. *Develop a financing strategy.* Develop a clear and comprehensive financing strategy outlining how you intend to secure the necessary funds. This may involve a combination of debt and equity financing, as well as other creative financing solutions tailored to your unique situation.

5. *Identify potential lenders or investors.* Reach out to potential lenders or investors who may be interested in financing the deal. This could include banks, financial institutions, private equity firms, venture capitalists, angel investors, or crowdfunding platforms.

6. *Submit financing applications.* Prepare and submit financing applications to selected lenders or investors. Be sure to provide all requested information and documentation in a timely and organized manner to facilitate the review process.

7. *Negotiate terms and conditions.* Once you receive financing offers, carefully review and negotiate the terms and conditions to ensure they align with your needs and objectives. Pay close attention to interest rates, repayment terms, collateral requirements, covenants, and any other relevant provisions.

8. *Complete due diligence.* Lenders or investors may conduct due diligence to assess the viability and risk of the deal. Be prepared to provide additional information and address any concerns or questions that may arise during this process.

9. *Finalize financing agreements.* Once all parties are satisfied with the terms and conditions, formalize the financing agreements by signing the necessary documentation. Ensure that all legal requirements are met and that the agreements are legally binding.

10. *Disburse funds and close the deal.* Upon finalizing the financing arrangements, the funds are typically disbursed to complete the transaction. This may involve transferring ownership of assets, paying off existing debts, or fulfilling other financial obligations as specified in the deal.

By following these steps, you can effectively secure the financing needed to finalize the deal and achieve your business objectives. It's important to approach the financing process strategically and diligently to ensure a successful outcome.

Finalizing Paperwork and Documentation

Finalizing paperwork and documentation is a crucial step in formalizing any deal or agreement. This process involves preparing, reviewing, and signing all necessary legal documents to ensure that the terms and conditions of the deal are clearly defined and legally binding. Here's a detailed guide on how to finalize paperwork and documentation:

1. *Compile required documents.* Gather all the necessary paperwork and documentation related to the deal. This may include contracts, agreements, financial statements, licenses, permits, certificates, and any other relevant documents.

2. *Review legal requirements.* Ensure that all documentation complies with applicable laws, regulations, and industry standards. Seek legal advice if necessary to confirm that the documents are legally sound and adequately protect the interests of all parties involved.

3. *Draft agreements and contracts.* Prepare formal agreements and contracts that outline the terms and conditions of the deal in clear and unambiguous language. Include details such as the parties involved, the scope of the agreement, obligations and responsibilities, payment terms, timelines, termination clauses, and any other relevant provisions.

4. *Negotiate terms.* Review the draft agreements with all parties involved and negotiate any terms or conditions that require clarification or modification. Reach consensus on all aspects of the deal before finalizing the documentation.

5. *Obtain signatures.* Once the agreements are finalized, arrange for all parties to sign the documents. This can be

done in person, electronically, or through authorized representatives, depending on the preferences and requirements of the parties involved.

6. *Witness or notarize documents.* Some documents may require witness signatures or notarization to validate their authenticity and enforceability. Arrange for these formalities to be completed as necessary.

7. *Distribute copies.* Provide copies of the signed documents to all parties involved for their records. Ensure that each party receives a complete set of documentation related to the deal.

8. *File documents.* Keep organized records of all finalized paperwork and documentation for future reference and compliance purposes. File the documents securely in a designated location where they can be easily accessed when needed.

9. *Implement obligations.* Review the terms outlined in the agreements and ensure that all parties understand their obligations and responsibilities. Take necessary steps to implement the terms of the deal according to the agreed-upon timelines and conditions.

10. *Monitor compliance.* Continuously monitor compliance with the terms of the agreements and address any issues or discrepancies that may arise promptly. Keep lines of communication open between all parties to ensure that the deal proceeds smoothly and as planned.

By following these steps, you can effectively finalize paperwork and documentation related to your deal, ensuring that all parties are legally bound by the agreed-upon terms and conditions. Thoroughness and attention to detail are essential to minimize the risk of misunderstandings or disputes in the future.

Obtaining Insurance

Obtaining insurance for a boat is essential to protect your investment and mitigate financial risks associated with potential accidents, damages, or liabilities. Here's a guide on how to obtain boat insurance:

1. *Evaluate your insurance needs.* Determine the type and amount of insurance coverage you need based on factors such as the type of boat you own, its value, how you plan to use it, and any legal requirements in your area.
2. *Research insurance providers.* Research insurance companies that offer boat insurance policies. Consider factors such as their reputation, financial stability, coverage options, customer service, and premiums.
3. *Understand coverage options.* Familiarize yourself with the different types of coverage options available for boat insurance:
   a. Property coverage: Covers damage to your boat, including collisions, theft, vandalism, and weather-related damage.
   b. Liability coverage: Protects you against financial responsibility for bodily injury or property damage caused by your boat to others.
   c. Medical payments coverage: Covers medical expenses for you and your passengers if injured in a boating accident.
   d. Uninsured/underinsured boater coverage: Provides protection if you're involved in an accident with another boater who has insufficient or no insurance.
   e. Towing and assistance coverage: Covers the cost of towing and emergency assistance services if your boat breaks down.

f. Personal effects coverage: Covers personal belongings on your boat, such as fishing equipment, electronics, and clothing.

4. *Request quotes.* Contact multiple insurance providers to request quotes for boat insurance based on your coverage needs and the specifics of your boat. Compare quotes to find the best coverage at a competitive price.

5. *Provide necessary information.* When applying for boat insurance, be prepared to provide information about your boat, such as its make, model, year, length, value, horsepower, safety features, and where it will be stored.

6. *Review policy terms and conditions.* Carefully review the terms and conditions of each insurance policy, including coverage limits, deductibles, exclusions, and any additional provisions. Ensure that you understand what is covered and what is not covered under the policy.

7. *Customize your policy.* Work with your insurance agent to customize your policy to suit your specific needs and preferences. Consider adding optional coverages or endorsements for additional protection, if necessary.

8. *Complete application and payment.* Once you've chosen a policy, complete the insurance application and submit any required documentation. Pay the initial premium to activate your coverage.

9. *Receive proof of insurance.* After your application is approved and payment is processed, you'll receive a proof of insurance document, typically in the form of an insurance policy or certificate. Keep this document in a safe place and carry it on your boat as proof of coverage.

10. *Review and update annually.* Review your boat insurance policy annually to ensure that it still meets your needs and provides adequate coverage. Update your policy as necessary to reflect any changes in your boat or boating activities.

By following these steps, you can obtain the necessary insurance coverage to protect your boat and enjoy peace of mind while out on the water. It's important to work with a reputable insurance provider and carefully review your policy to ensure that you have the coverage you need.

Arranging for Delivery or Transport

Arranging delivery or transport for a boat involves careful planning and coordination to ensure the safe and efficient transportation of the vessel from one location to another. Whether you're purchasing a new boat, relocating an existing one, or transporting it for maintenance or storage, here's a guide on how to arrange for delivery or transport:

1. *Determine transport needs.* Assess your transport needs based on factors such as the size, type, and weight of the boat, as well as the distance and route of transportation. Determine whether you need overland transport via trailer or water transport via a shipping vessel.
2. *Research transport options.* Research and compare different transport options available in your area. This may include hiring professional boat transport companies, utilizing boat transport brokers, or arranging transportation through private individuals or yacht clubs.
3. *Get quotes.* Contact multiple transport providers to request quotes based on your specific transport requirements. Provide detailed information about the boat, pickup and delivery locations, travel dates, and any special considerations or requirements.
4. *Verify credentials and insurance.* Before hiring a transport provider, verify their credentials, licenses, insurance coverage, and reputation. Ensure that they have the necessary experience and expertise to handle the transportation of your boat safely and legally.

5. *Plan pickup and delivery.* Coordinate with the transport provider to schedule pickup of the boat from its current location and delivery to its destination. Determine the most convenient dates and times for both parties and confirm the logistics of the transportation process.

6. *Prepare the boat.* Prepare the boat for transportation according to the transport provider's instructions. This may include securing loose items, removing valuables and personal belongings, draining fluids, disconnecting batteries, and securing hatches and openings.

7. *Coordinate permits and regulations.* Ensure that all necessary permits, licenses, and regulatory requirements are met for transporting the boat, especially if crossing state lines or international borders. Obtain any required permits or documentation in advance to avoid delays or legal issues.

8. *Monitor transport progress.* Stay in communication with the transport provider throughout the transportation process to monitor progress and address any concerns or issues that may arise. Obtain updates on the location and status of the boat during transit.

9. Inspect upon arrival: Upon delivery of the boat to its destination, inspect it carefully for any damage or discrepancies. Document any issues or concerns and communicate them to the transport provider immediately.

10. *Complete payment and documentation.* Once the boat has been safely delivered, complete payment to the transport provider according to the agreed-upon terms. Obtain any necessary documentation, such as a bill of lading or delivery receipt, to confirm the successful transport of the boat.

By following these steps, you can effectively arrange for the delivery or transport of your boat with confidence, ensuring a smooth and hassle-free transportation process. It's important to work with reputable and experienced transport providers to safeguard the integrity of your vessel and ensure its safe arrival at its destination.

Chapter 9
POSTPURCHASE CONSIDERATIONS

Arranging for Maintenance and Repairs

Arranging for maintenance and repairs for your boat is essential to keep it in top condition and ensure safe and enjoyable boating experiences. Here's a guide on how to arrange for boat maintenance and repairs:

1. *Identify maintenance needs.* Regular maintenance is crucial for preserving the condition and performance of your boat. Identify any maintenance tasks that need to be performed based on manufacturer recommendations, usage patterns, and visual inspections.
2. *Prioritize repairs.* Assess the condition of your boat and prioritize any repairs that are necessary to address safety concerns or prevent further damage. Make a list of repairs needed, categorizing them based on urgency and severity.
3. *Research service providers.* Research and identify reputable service providers in your area that specialize in boat maintenance and repairs. This may include marinas, boatyards, marine mechanics, and authorized dealers for your boat's brand.
4. *Check credentials and reputation.* Verify the credentials, certifications, and reputation of potential service providers.

Look for reviews and testimonials from previous customers to ensure they have a track record of quality workmanship and customer satisfaction.

5. *Request estimates.* Contact multiple service providers to request estimates for the maintenance and repairs needed for your boat. Provide detailed information about the make, model, and condition of your boat to ensure accurate quotes.

6. *Schedule service appointments.* Once you've selected a service provider, schedule service appointments for the maintenance and repairs. Coordinate with the provider to find convenient dates and times for dropping off and picking up your boat.

7. *Communicate requirements.* Clearly communicate your maintenance and repair requirements to the service provider. Provide any documentation or information they may need, such as service manuals, warranty information, and details about the issues you've observed.

8. *Authorize work.* Before any work begins, review and authorize the proposed maintenance and repairs. Ensure that you understand the scope of work, associated costs, and estimated completion timeline. Discuss any questions or concerns with the service provider before giving approval.

9. *Monitor progress.* Stay in communication with the service provider throughout the maintenance and repair process to monitor progress and address any unexpected issues or delays that may arise. Request updates as needed to keep informed about the status of the work.

10. *Inspect completed work.* Once the maintenance and repairs are complete, inspect the work thoroughly to ensure that all tasks have been performed to your satisfaction. Test the boat's systems and components to verify that everything is functioning properly.

11. *Complete payment and documentation.* After verifying the quality of the work, complete payment to the service provider according to the agreed-upon terms. Obtain any nec-

essary documentation, such as invoices, receipts, and service reports, for your records.

12. *Schedule regular maintenance.* Establish a schedule for regular maintenance tasks to keep your boat in optimal condition over time. This may include routine inspections, engine servicing, hull cleaning, and other preventive maintenance activities.

By following these steps, you can effectively arrange for the maintenance and repairs needed to keep your boat in excellent condition and ensure many years of safe and enjoyable boating adventures. Regular maintenance and timely repairs are key to protecting your investment and maximizing the life span of your boat.

Learning Safe Boating Practices

Learning safe boating practices is essential for ensuring the safety of yourself, your passengers, and others on the water. Here's a comprehensive guide on how to learn safe boating practices:

1. *Take a boating safety course.* Enroll in a boating safety course offered by organizations such as the US Coast Guard Auxiliary, the US Power Squadrons, or state boating agencies. These courses cover essential topics such as navigation rules, boat handling, emergency procedures, and boating laws.

2. *Study boating safety resources.* Familiarize yourself with boating safety guidelines and resources provided by reputable organizations such as the US Coast Guard, the National Safe Boating Council, and the American Boating Association. These resources include handbooks, guides, videos, and online tutorials.

3. *Know the rules and regulations.* Learn and understand the boating laws, rules, and regulations applicable to the area where you'll be boating. This includes navigation rules,

speed limits, buoy markers, licensing requirements, and safety equipment regulations.

4. *Practice safe boat operation.* Learn how to operate your boat safely and confidently by practicing basic maneuvers such as starting, stopping, steering, docking, and navigating in various conditions. Take the time to become familiar with the controls and handling characteristics of your boat.

5. *Understand weather conditions.* Stay informed about current and forecasted weather conditions before heading out on the water. Learn how to interpret weather forecasts, recognize signs of changing weather patterns, and respond appropriately to adverse weather conditions.

6. *Wear a life jacket.* Always wear a properly fitting US Coast Guard–approved life jacket when boating, regardless of your swimming ability or the type of boat you're on. Ensure that life jackets are readily accessible and properly maintained for all passengers on board.

7. *Avoid alcohol and drugs.* Never operate a boat under the influence of alcohol or drugs, as impaired boating significantly increases the risk of accidents, injuries, and fatalities. Designate a sober skipper and encourage responsible behavior among all passengers.

8. *Practice boating courtesy.* Show respect and consideration for other boaters, swimmers, anglers, and wildlife by practicing boating courtesy and adhering to navigation rules. Maintain a safe distance from other vessels, reduce speed in congested areas, and avoid creating excessive wake or noise.

9. *Be prepared for emergencies.* Equip your boat with essential safety equipment and emergency supplies, including life jackets, a first aid kit, a fire extinguisher, signaling devices, navigation lights, and a throwable flotation device. Know how to use this equipment and respond effectively to emergencies such as capsizing, grounding, or engine failure.

10. *Stay informed and updated.* Stay informed about boating safety best practices, regulations, and advancements by regularly attending boating safety seminars, workshops, and

refresher courses. Stay updated on changes in boating laws and regulations that may affect your boating activities.

11. *Lead by example.* Set a positive example for others by practicing safe boating habits and promoting a culture of safety among your family, friends, and fellow boaters. Encourage everyone onboard to follow boating safety guidelines and take responsibility for their actions.

12. *Stay alert and vigilant.* Stay attentive, alert, and vigilant while boating, maintaining a proper lookout for hazards, obstacles, and other vessels. Avoid distractions such as excessive speed, loud music, or using electronic devices while underway.

By following these steps and committing to ongoing education and practice, you can become a responsible and confident boater who prioritizes safety on the water. Remember that safe boating is a shared responsibility that requires cooperation, awareness, and preparedness from everyone on board.

Joining Boating Communities and Clubs

There are numerous boating communities and clubs around the world where you can join like-minded individuals who share a passion for boating. These communities offer opportunities for socializing, learning, and participating in boating-related activities. Here are some types of boating communities and clubs you might consider joining:

1. Yacht clubs: Yacht clubs are prestigious organizations typically located near bodies of water. They offer various amenities such as marinas, boat storage facilities, dining options, and social events. Yacht clubs cater to sailors and powerboat enthusiasts alike and often host regattas, races, and cruising events.

2. Sailing clubs: Sailing clubs focus specifically on the sport of sailing and are open to sailors of all skill levels, from begin-

ners to experienced racers. These clubs provide opportunities for sailing instruction, racing, socializing, and cruising. Many sailing clubs offer sailing lessons and certification programs.

3. Powerboat clubs: Powerboat clubs cater to owners and enthusiasts of motorized boats, including cruisers, speedboats, and fishing boats. These clubs organize events such as boat rallies, poker runs, fishing tournaments, and social gatherings for members to enjoy.

4. Boat owner associations: Boat owner associations bring together individuals who own specific types of boats, such as sailboats, powerboats, or fishing boats. These associations provide resources, support, and camaraderie among boat owners, often focusing on specific brands or models of boats.

5. Community boating organizations: Community boating organizations aim to make boating accessible to a broader audience by offering affordable boating programs, lessons, and rentals. These organizations often focus on promoting boating safety, education, and environmental stewardship.

6. Cruising clubs: Cruising clubs are ideal for boaters who enjoy long-distance cruising and exploring different destinations by boat. These clubs organize group cruises, rendezvous, and social events for members to share experiences and travel together.

7. Fishing clubs: Fishing clubs bring together anglers who share a passion for fishing and boating. These clubs organize fishing tournaments, outings, and seminars on various fishing techniques and strategies.

8. Kayak and canoe clubs: If you prefer paddling sports, consider joining a kayak or canoe club. These clubs offer opportunities for paddlers to explore rivers, lakes, and coastal waters, participate in group paddles, and learn new skills.

9. Boating meetup groups: Online platforms like Meetup.com often host boating-related meetup groups where boat-

ers can connect, organize outings, and share knowledge and experiences.

When choosing a boating community or club to join, consider factors such as the club's location, facilities, membership requirements, activities, and the interests of its members. Visit club websites, attend open houses or events, and talk to current members to learn more about what each club has to offer before making a decision.

Enjoying Your New Boat!

Enjoying your new boat is an exciting and rewarding experience that allows you to explore the open water, relax with friends and family, and create lasting memories. Here are some tips for maximizing your enjoyment of your new boat:

1. *Familiarize yourself with your boat.* Take the time to thoroughly familiarize yourself with your new boat, including its features, controls, and safety equipment. Review the owner's manual and take a boating safety course if necessary.
2. *Plan fun excursions.* Plan fun and adventurous excursions to take advantage of your boat's capabilities. Explore nearby waterways, visit scenic destinations, and try out different activities such as fishing, swimming, waterskiing, or snorkeling.
3. *Invite friends and family.* Share the joy of boating with friends and family by inviting them to join you on your outings. Organize picnics, barbecues, or sunset cruises to make the experience even more enjoyable.
4. *Discover new destinations.* Use your boat as a means of exploration to discover new destinations and hidden gems along the coastline or on inland waterways. Research interesting places to visit and chart your course accordingly.
5. *Join boating events and clubs.* Participate in boating events, regattas, and rendezvous organized by local boating clubs or associations. These events provide opportunities to meet

other boaters, share experiences, and enjoy camaraderie on the water.

6. *Try different activities.* Experiment with different boating activities to find what you enjoy most. Whether it's cruising, fishing, watersports, or simply anchoring in a secluded cove, there's something for everyone to enjoy on the water.

7. *Practice good seamanship.* Practice good seamanship and boating etiquette to ensure a safe and enjoyable experience for yourself and others on the water. Follow navigation rules, maintain a proper lookout, and operate your boat responsibly at all times.

8. *Stay safe.* Prioritize safety by wearing life jackets, familiarizing yourself with local boating regulations, and staying alert to potential hazards on the water. Be prepared for emergencies by carrying essential safety equipment and knowing how to use it.

9. *Maintain your boat.* Keep your boat well-maintained to ensure its reliability and performance. Follow recommended maintenance schedules, perform regular inspections, and address any issues promptly to prevent problems down the line.

10. *Document your adventures.* Capture and document your boating adventures through photos, videos, or a boating journal. Reflect on your experiences and cherish the memories you create with your boat.

11. *Respect the environment.* Practice environmental stewardship by minimizing your impact on the marine environment. Dispose of waste properly, avoid disturbing wildlife, and follow designated boating channels to protect sensitive habitats.

12. *Relax and enjoy.* Above all, relax and enjoy the freedom and tranquility that boating offers. Take time to soak in the beauty of nature, unwind from the stresses of everyday life, and savor the moments spent on the water with loved ones.

By following these tips, you can make the most of your new boat and create unforgettable experiences that will enrich your life for years to come. Whether you're cruising, fishing, or simply enjoying the scenery, boating offers endless opportunities for adventure and relaxation.

Chapter 10
CONCLUSION

Recap of Key Points

Of course, here's a recap of the key points for enjoying your new boat:

1. *Familiarize yourself.* Take the time to learn about your boat's features, controls, and safety equipment.
2. *Plan excursions.* Plan fun outings to explore new destinations and try out different activities on the water.
3. *Invite others.* Share the joy of boating by inviting friends and family to join you on your adventures.
4. *Discover new places.* Use your boat to discover new destinations and hidden gems along the coastline or on inland waterways.
5. *Join boating events.* Participate in boating events and clubs to meet other boaters and enjoy camaraderie on the water.
6. *Try different activities.* Experiment with various boating activities to find what you enjoy most, whether it's cruising, fishing, or watersports.
7. *Practice good seamanship.* Prioritize safety and responsible boating practices to ensure a safe and enjoyable experience for everyone onboard.
8. *Maintain your boat.* Keep your boat well-maintained to ensure its reliability and performance over time.

9. *Document your adventures.* Capture and document your boating adventures to cherish the memories for years to come.
10. *Respect the environment.* Practice environmental stewardship by minimizing your impact on the marine environment and respecting wildlife.
11. *Relax and enjoy.* Take time to relax and enjoy the freedom and tranquility that boating offers.

By keeping these key points in mind, you can make the most of your boating experience and create unforgettable memories on the water.

Final Tips for First-Time Boat Buyers

Here are some final tips for first-time boat buyers to consider:

1. *Research thoroughly.* Take your time to research different types of boats, their features, and their intended uses. Consider factors such as size, type, power, and amenities to find the right boat for your needs.
2. *Set a budget.* Determine your budget for purchasing and owning a boat, taking into account not only the initial purchase price but also ongoing expenses such as maintenance, insurance, storage, and fuel.
3. *Consider used boats.* Don't overlook the option of buying a used boat, as it can often offer better value for money than purchasing new. Just be sure to thoroughly inspect the boat and consider getting a marine survey before making a purchase.
4. *Take a test drive.* Before committing to a purchase, take the boat for a test drive on the water to assess its performance, handling, and overall condition. This will give you a better idea of whether it meets your expectations and needs.

5. *Get proper training.* If you're new to boating, consider taking a boating safety course and/or getting professional instruction on boat handling and safety. This will help you feel more confident and comfortable on the water and reduce the risk of accidents.

6. *Understand ownership costs.* Be aware of the full cost of boat ownership beyond the initial purchase price. Factor in expenses such as maintenance, insurance, storage, fuel, registration, and taxes to ensure you can afford to own and operate a boat.

7. *Plan for storage.* Decide where you'll store your boat when it's not in use, whether it's at a marina, a storage facility, on a trailer, or at your own dock. Consider the costs, convenience, and amenities offered by different storage options.

8. *Invest in safety equipment.* Prioritize safety by equipping your boat with essential safety equipment such as life jackets, navigation lights, fire extinguishers, distress signals, and a first aid kit. Ensure that all safety equipment is in good working condition and easily accessible.

9. *Build a network.* Connect with other boaters and join boating communities or clubs to learn from their experiences, get advice, and share resources. Building a network of fellow boaters can enhance your boating experience and provide valuable support.

10. *Enjoy the journey.* Finally, remember that boating is meant to be enjoyable and relaxing. Take the time to savor the experience of being out on the water, exploring new destinations, and creating lasting memories with friends and family.

By following these tips, first-time boat buyers can make informed decisions, enjoy a smooth purchasing process, and embark on a rewarding journey as boat owners.

Chapter 11
QUESTIONS TO ASK THE SELLER/BROKER WHEN BUYING A BOAT

When buying a boat, it's crucial to gather as much information as possible to make an informed decision. Here are some important questions you should consider asking the seller or broker:

1. Ownership and title
   - Can you provide proof of ownership?
   - Is the title clear of any liens or encumbrances?
2. History and usage
   - What is the history of the boat (e.g., number of previous owners, any accidents or major repairs)?
   - How has the boat been used (e.g., freshwater/saltwater, recreational/fishing)?
3. Maintenance and storage
   - Can you provide maintenance records for the boat?
   - Where has the boat been stored?
4. Condition and inspection
   - Can I have a professional survey and a mechanical inspection performed?
   - Are there any known issues or needed repairs with the boat?

5. Inclusions
   - What is included in the sale of the boat (e.g., trailers, equipment, accessories)?
   - Are there any warranties or guarantees still in effect?
6. Performance and handling
   - How does the boat handle in different conditions?
   - Can we take the boat for a sea trial?
7. Financial and legal
   - What are the terms of the sale?
   - Are there any outstanding fees or taxes due?
8. Documentation and manuals
   - Are all the manuals and documentation available?
   - Is there a logbook of past voyages?
9. Upgrades and modifications
   - Have any upgrades or modifications been made to the boat?
   - Were these upgrades professionally done, and are there receipts or warranties for the work?
10. Safety and equipment
    - Does the boat come with all the necessary safety equipment?
    - Is the safety equipment up to date and in good working order?
    Remember, the specific questions can vary depending on the type of boat you are interested in (sailboat, motorboat, yacht, etc.), its size, and intended use. It's always a good idea to be thorough and perhaps consult a professional if you're not experienced with boats.
11. Engine and propulsion
    - How many hours are on the engine(s)?
    - When was the last engine service, and can you show the service records?
    - Are there any known issues with the engine or propulsion system?

12. Electronics and navigation
    - Are the onboard electronics and navigation systems fully functional?
    - Are there any recent upgrades to the electronics?
    - How is the wiring, and are there any known electrical issues?
13. Hull and structure
    - When was the last time the hull was inspected out of water?
    - Is there any evidence of blistering, cracking, or repair on the hull?
    - Are there any known structural concerns with the deck or hull?
14. Cosmetics and comfort
    - What is the condition of the upholstery and interior cabin areas?
    - Are there any signs of water damage or mold inside the boat?
    - How is the condition of the canvas, bimini tops, or enclosures?
15. Safety certifications
    - Does the boat meet all the current safety regulations?
    - When was the last safety inspection performed?
16. Fuel efficiency and range
    - What is the boat's fuel efficiency like?
    - How large is the fuel tank, and what range can be expected on a full tank?
17. Manufacturing and model
    - What year was the boat manufactured, and what is the make and model?
    - Are there any known recalls or common issues with this particular model?
18. Dinghy and tender
    - Is there a dinghy or tender included with the boat?
    - What is the condition of the dinghy, and does it have its own motor?

19. Mooring and storage
    - Will the current mooring be available to the new owner?
    - What are the costs associated with the boat's current storage or mooring?
20. Transfer of ownership
    - What is the process for transferring ownership?
    - Are there any transfer fees or duties that need to be paid?
21. Insurance
    - What kind of insurance is on the boat, and is it transferable to the new owner?
    - Can you recommend any marine insurance companies?
22. Reason for sale
    - Why are you selling the boat?
    - Is there a timeline in which you are hoping to complete the sale?

Remember to not only rely on verbal responses but also ask for any available documentation that supports the seller's claims. If possible, bring an experienced boater or a marine surveyor with you to help assess the boat's condition and value.

Chapter 12
QUESTIONS WE WISH WE'D ASKED

Had we known what to ask at the start of our journey to find our first boat, it would have included:

Insights for Novice Boat Buyers: Lessons Learned

Embarking on boat ownership is an adventure filled with unique lessons. Here's some distilled wisdom from experienced owners to guide you through:

1. Boat ownership is personal. Prioritize your needs over others' opinions. Each owner values different features based on their individual preferences.
2. Adventure horizons: Keep your starting point flexible. Global opportunities abound, like finding a seasoned ocean cruiser in places like the Panama Canal, where boaters often sell after completing significant passages.
3. Experience variety: Spend time on as many boats as possible. Cruising or simply observing different vessels helps clarify what's essential for your journey.
4. Crew considerations: Determine if you need a vessel suitable for solo or two-person navigation early on, impacting the required size, equipment, and onboard systems.

5. Essential features: Stand firm on what you deem critical. The market has more boats than buyers, so you needn't compromise on key features.
6. Financial boundaries: Remember, boats are costly to maintain. It's wise to have a generous financial buffer, possibly two or three times your initial estimate.
7. Document everything: Capture images of every part of the boat for reference.
8. Inquisitive mindset: Don't hesitate to ask questions. It's crucial for making an informed decision (refer to our suggested questions list).
9. Understand depreciation: Acknowledge that a boat is not a financial investment but a commitment to a passion that comes with ongoing costs.
10. Size and cost correlation: Larger boats mean larger expenses for both docking and maintenance. Evaluate the necessity of additional space.
11. Guest accommodations: Consider if extra space for guests is a necessity. Sometimes, less space means more intimacy and less hassle.
12. In-depth inspection: Examine the inner workings thoroughly: engine, electrical systems, rudder, safety gear, and energy systems. Perform a comprehensive check.
13. Project vs. pleasure: Decide if you're ready for a fixer-upper with potential long-term projects or if you prefer an immediate cruising experience without the wait.
14. Navigational plans: Consider your immediate and future navigational activities. Are you planning to cruise internationally, live aboard, enjoy coastal journeys, participate in races, or traverse oceans?
15. Value perception in deals: A good transaction often leaves the buyer feeling they could have paid less and the seller thinking they could have earned more.

This advice aims to prepare you for the realities of boat ownership and help you make decisions that align with your cruising dreams and practical considerations.

Chapter 13
BOAT LINGO

1. *BOAT* stands for "break out another thousand."
2. The classic ride of shame—that's when your boat is getting towed
3. "Break out another couple of tens of thousands!"—that is when you need a new engine because someone getting a great deal on a used boat with only a few hundred hours on an engine later that season has the engine completely fail due to long-deferred maintenance.
4. Marine age – The time an engine and boat systems sat with saltwater in or around them
5. Ten percent of the purchase price – Take the new value of your old boat and assume you're going to spend 10 percent of that cost in maintenance every year.
6. Purchase of a depreciating asset – Your boat loses some percentage of its value the minute you bring it home and then greater percentages year after year.
7. Summer slip – Getting a summer slip for a boat refers to renting a space at a marina or dock where you can moor your boat for the summer season. This slip is essentially your boat's parking spot in the water. Marinas offer various facilities that can include security, electricity hookups, water supply, and sometimes amenities like showers or laundry facilities. Renting a summer slip is a convenient option for boat owners who want easy access to their vessel without the hassle of launching and retrieving it every time

they want to go out on the water. It also provides a secure location for the boat when not in use.

8. Winter storage – Winter storage for a boat involves keeping your boat in a safe location during the winter months when it's not in use due to colder weather and potentially icy water conditions. This can include dry storage on land in a boatyard, storage in a covered facility, or sometimes in-water storage in special climates where freezing isn't a concern. The main goal is to protect the boat from the harsh winter weather, which can cause damage to its structure and systems. Winter storage often involves winterization processes as well, such as draining water from the engine and plumbing, adding antifreeze, and covering the boat to keep it clean and dry.

9. Winterizing the boat – Winterizing a powered boat is a crucial process to prepare and protect it for the cold weather months, ensuring that it remains in good condition and is ready to use when spring arrives. The process typically involves several key steps:

   1. *Engine care.* This includes changing the oil and oil filter to remove contaminants and moisture that could cause corrosion. Antifreeze may be added to the cooling system to prevent any remaining water from freezing and causing damage.

   2. *Fuel system.* The fuel tank is often filled to minimize the space for condensation to form, potentially adding a fuel stabilizer to prevent the fuel from deteriorating over time.

   3. *Battery maintenance.* Batteries are usually disconnected, removed, and stored in a cool, dry place where they can be kept charged over the winter.

   4. Draining water: All water is drained from the engine, plumbing, and any onboard systems to prevent freezing damage. Nontoxic antifreeze is then added to the plumbing systems to protect them.

5.   Cleaning: The boat is thoroughly cleaned inside and out to remove salt, dirt, and debris. This helps prevent corrosion and mold growth.
6.   Covering: A cover is placed over the boat to protect it from the elements, like snow and rain, and to keep it clean.
7.   Lubrication: Moving parts, such as hinges and latches, are lubricated to prevent them from seizing up over the winter.
8.   Inspecting and repairing: This is also a good time to inspect the boat for any damage or wear and address these issues before storage.

Each step in the winterization process is designed to address the challenges of inactivity and cold weather, helping to ensure the boat's longevity and reducing the risk of costly repairs.

Author's Note

In the early days of my nautical adventures, the ocean was a vast, undulating mystery, its secrets hidden beneath waves that seemed as daunting as they were mesmerizing. My initiation into this watery world was not without its trials; seasickness clung to me like a stubborn barnacle for a decade, testing my resolve and passion for the sea. Yet perseverance is a powerful tide, and eventually, I overcame this malady, setting my sights on a dream that had gestated in the depths of my heart: to own a boat.

My first vessel was a modest Grady White, a twenty-foot craft with a small cuddy cabin that, despite its narrow beam, was a beacon of freedom on the open water. It was my floating sanctuary, a place where I could escape the mundane and embrace the unpredictable dance of the sea. For a few years, I piloted my Grady White through countless journeys, each expedition etching invaluable experiences into my sailor's soul.

However, as time unfurled its sails, I began to recognize the limitations of my beloved boat. What once felt like boundless freedom now seemed confined by invisible chains. The Grady White, while perfect for serene days within the sheltered embrace of Barnegat Bay, was ill-suited for the ambitions that grew within me. I yearned to chase horizons beyond the bay to fish in the bountiful but treacherous waters miles offshore, yet my small vessel was not made for such dreams.

Venturing into the ocean required a cautious dance with the weather and sea conditions, a constant calculation of risk and reward. The narrow beam of my boat, combined with its limited fuel capacity and reliance on a single engine, felt like a delicate thread holding me to the safety of the shore. The thought of the engine failing in the vastness of the ocean, far from help, was a specter that haunted my expeditions. And though my VHF radio was a lifeline, the fear lingered—would it be strong enough to summon aid should I find myself adrift?

This realization, born from a blend of love and limitation, led me to a crossroads. The sea, with its infinite lessons, taught me that growth often requires letting go. My Grady White had been the vessel of my initiation, a companion through seas both calm and stormy. But to pursue the dreams that swelled like the tides within me, I knew I needed a vessel that could carry me beyond the constraints of my current reality.

The decision to seek a new boat was bittersweet. Parting with my Grady White felt like saying farewell to an old friend, a keeper of memories and milestones. Yet the horizon called to me with a siren's song, promising adventures that lay just beyond my reach. Armed with the experiences gained and lessons learned, I embarked on the next chapter of my boating journey, guided by the stars and driven by the relentless pursuit of the unknown.

As I ventured farther from the safety of the bay, each wave a testament to the journey behind and the vast expanse ahead, I realized that the sea is both a teacher and a temptress. It challenges us to confront our fears, to push beyond our perceived limits, and to embrace the adventure that lies in the unknown. And though the boat under my feet may change, my heart remains anchored to the sea, forever chasing the horizon.

As years unfurled like sails against the wind, my life took on new dimensions. The arrival of my family brought a joy and fulfillment that surpassed my wildest dreams, and with them, I wanted to share the boundless beauty of the sea. The Grady White, my first leap into the world of boating, had become a vessel of cherished memories but was no longer suited to the expanding horizons of our collective adventures. It was time for a change, a step toward a future where we could all embark on journeys together, exploring farther, embracing the vastness of the ocean as one.

The transition to a twenty-seven-foot Sea Ray symbolized this new chapter. It was a vessel that promised comfort for my family and the ability to cruise the waters with ease. We spent countless days gliding over the waves, the laughter of my loved ones mingling with the rhythmic song of the sea. Those years are etched in my heart, a testament to the joy that comes from sharing one's passions with the people closest to them. Yet as time marched on, the whispers of the deep sea called to me, a siren song urging me to venture farther, to seek out the solitary peace that comes from fishing in the vast expanse of the ocean.

The Sea Ray, for all its comforts and shared memories, could not fulfill this growing desire within me. Its narrow beam and limited fuel capacity were not designed for the rugged demands of deep-sea fishing. My needs had evolved, and with them, my vessel must too. Thus, I bid farewell to the Sea Ray, trading it for a thirty-six-foot Luhrs sportfish. This new boat was a beacon of possibilities, equipped with a three-hundred-gallon fuel tank and a thirteen-foot beam that provided the stability and range I craved. It was a vessel that could carry us not just across the water but into the future, allowing us to fish or cruise further into the ocean with confidence and space to breathe.

Navigating this larger craft into waters twenty and thirty miles offshore became my new challenge, a task I undertook with the same fervor that had driven me to conquer seasickness so many years ago. It took years to feel truly at ease at the helm, to understand the nuances of handling such a powerful vessel in the unpredictable embrace of the sea. Yet even as I grew more comfortable, my dreams expanded beyond the horizon. The canyons, lying about one hundred miles or more from shore, called to me. These deep, mysterious parts of the ocean promised fishing and adventures that I had only dared to imagine.

The lure of the canyons was irresistible, yet I was acutely aware of the risks involved. The weather in those remote parts of the ocean was unpredictable, often treacherous. To pursue this dream, I needed not just a capable boat, but also a wealth of knowledge, preparation, and respect for the sea's might. It was a pursuit that demanded more than just passion; it required wisdom, patience, and an unwavering commitment to safety.

As I began to prepare for these distant voyages, my heart swelled with a mixture of excitement and solemnity. The sea had always been my teacher, guiding me through lessons of humility, resilience, and the profound beauty of nature. To venture into the canyons was to embark on a journey not just of physical distance, but of personal growth. It was a testament to the enduring call of the sea, a call that had shaped my life in ways I could never have imagined.

In this new chapter, the sea awaited, its depths filled with unknown challenges and treasures. With my family by my side, my Luhrs ready to brave the open waters, and my heart open to the lessons ahead, I steered toward the canyons, ready to embrace whatever adventures lay beyond the horizon. The journey was not just about reaching a destination but about the continual pursuit of dreams, the courage to face the unknown, and the unbreakable bond between a sailor and the sea.

The allure of the canyon, with its unpredictable weather and the promise of unparalleled fishing, had become an indelible part of my life. Each journey to these distant waters was an adventure, a balance of risk and reward where the elements themselves dictated the terms of our voyage. The Luhrs, my trusted vessel, had carried us far, braving the deep blue expanse to reach the fishing grounds that lay a hundred miles from shore. These expeditions were not without their challenges, each one teaching me more about the sea and about myself.

However, as our journeys to the canyon became more frequent, new concerns began to surface. The realization that our fuel tanks neared emptiness upon returning to shore brought a discomfort I could not ignore. The vast ocean, which had always been a source of freedom and adventure, now underscored our vulnerability. The thought of being stranded without fuel, far from any help, was a stark reminder of the ocean's unforgiving nature.

Moreover, the size of our boat, a mere thirty-six feet in length, seemed increasingly insignificant against the backdrop of the open sea. Out there, amid the rolling waves and vast swells, our vessel felt like a mere speck against the vastness of the ocean. The constant rocking from side to side, while manageable, was far from comfortable, adding to the sense of trepidation that began to accompany our trips.

It was this growing unease that led me to consider an addition to our nautical arsenal. The idea of acquiring a center console equipped with three Mercury Verado outboard engines presented a tantalizing solution. Such a boat, with its sleek design and powerful engines, could traverse the distance to the canyon in significantly less time. On a perfect day, it could cruise at an astonishing fifty miles per hour, a stark contrast to the Luhrs, which, even at its best, could only manage twenty-five miles per hour.

The prospect of making the journey more efficiently, with reduced fuel concerns and a quicker response to changing weather conditions, was compelling. A center console would offer not just speed, but also a sense of security, mitigating the fear of running out of fuel or being caught unprepared by sudden storms. Yet this was not a decision to be made lightly. Such an investment required careful consideration, weighing the benefits of speed and efficiency against the cost and practicality of maintaining two boats.

As I pondered this decision, I reflected on the journey that had brought me to this point. From my early days overcoming seasickness to navigating the challenges of deep-sea fishing, each step had been a lesson in adaptability and resilience. The sea had taught me to respect its power, to prepare meticulously, and to embrace change as a constant companion.

In contemplating the addition of a center console, I saw not just a strategic move but a continuation of my evolution as a sailor. It was an acknowledgment that the pursuit of passion often requires adaptation, a willingness to explore new solutions in the face of changing circumstances. Whether cruising with my family or braving the deep waters of the canyon, the essence of boating remained the same: a quest for connection with the sea, a journey of discovery that challenges and rewards in equal measure.

As I looked toward the horizon, contemplating the adventures that lay ahead, I knew that whatever decision I made would be guided by the lessons learned from the sea. In navigating the unknown, whether in life or on the water, the journey itself is the greatest destination, filled with moments of joy, challenge, and profound beauty.

The decision to invest in a thirty-eight-foot Fountain with triple 275 horsepower Verado engines marked a pivotal moment in my nautical journey. This sleek, powerful vessel became the embodiment of my desire to conquer the sea with speed, efficiency, and grace. On days when the weather gods smiled upon us, we would set off at dawn, cutting through the waves with unmatched velocity, bound for the distant fishing grounds of the canyon. The Fountain allowed us to cover an astonishing three hundred miles in a single day, a feat that brought both thrill and a sense of accomplishment, knowing we still had enough fuel to return safely to shore.

This period of my life was characterized by an insatiable appetite for the sea, a passion that extended beyond the familiar waters of New Jersey. Fortune smiled upon me, presenting opportunities to fish in the vibrant and diverse marine environments of the Florida Keys and the Fort Lauderdale area. My obsession with boating and fishing manifested in the acquisition of three additional vessels, each serving a unique purpose in my growing fleet.

In the serene waters of the Florida Keys, a forty-foot ocean yacht became my floating home for overnight excursions to Fort Jefferson, a historical gem located seventy miles southwest of Key West. These trips offered a blend of adventure and solitude, a chance to disconnect from the world and immerse myself in the natural beauty of the sea.

For days when the allure of inshore fishing called, I turned to a thirty-foot Scarab, powered by twin Yamaha 200 horsepower engines. This boat was perfectly suited for navigating the shallower waters, where the dance of light and shadow revealed the rich biodiversity of the coastal habitats.

My life had become a seamless blend of work, family, and boating. Every spare moment was dedicated to the sea, a testament to my deepening connection with the water and the vessels that carried me across its vast expanse. It was a natural progression, then, to seek formal recognition of my skills and experience. Obtaining my six-pack captain's license was not just a milestone; it was a commitment to excellence and safety, a badge of honor that acknowledged my dedication to the craft of boating.

As time passed, the evolution of my boating adventures continued. The Fountain, once the crown jewel of my New Jersey expeditions, was replaced with a thirty-two-foot SeaVee, a vessel that promised new adventures and challenges. The Fountain found a new home in Fort Lauderdale, a fitting stage for its prowess, where the fishing grounds beckoned with new mysteries to unravel.

This journey, from the initial days of battling seasickness to commanding a fleet of specialized vessels, reflects a life lived in harmony with the sea. Each boat, each voyage, was a chapter in a larger story of exploration, learning, and passion. The sea, with its ever-changing moods and boundless horizons, continued to teach me valuable lessons about respect, preparation, and the joy of discovery.

As I navigated the waters of life, balancing the demands of medical work as a physician and family with my love for boating, I found in the sea a reflection of my own evolving journey. It was a source of challenge and comfort, a space where dreams were pursued and sometimes, amid the quiet of a sunset over calm waters, realized. In embracing the call of the sea, I discovered not just the thrill of the chase but the profound satisfaction of a life lived with purpose, passion, and a relentless pursuit of the horizon. As one of the outcomes, I have pursued my passion in writing and have already dedicated two books to the interest of mariners.

The culmination of years spent on the water, learning its ways and embracing its lessons, led me to the realization of my ultimate dream: the acquisition of a sixty-foot powered catamaran. This vessel, which I affectionately named *Sea Scape*, was not just a boat; it was a floating testament to the passion and dedication that had fueled my journey from the outset. With a twenty-five-foot beam, *Sea Scape* was a marvel of nautical engineering, equipped with two robust Caterpillar engines, dual generators, a water maker, and an ice maker, setting a new standard for luxury and capability at sea.

The catamaran's design incorporated all the navigational instruments one could wish for, making it a navigator's dream. It boasted five staterooms, offering unparalleled comfort and privacy for my family and guests. The full galley, complete with a dishwasher and an oven that could accommodate baking on board, transformed *Sea Scape* into a home away from home. This vessel was built not just for cruising but for living.

I customized *Sea Scape* for fishing, adding rod holders and fighting stands on the pontoons at the stern, allowing it to seamlessly transition into a formidable fishing platform. This adaptability made the catamaran an ideal companion for my adventures, embodying the spirit of exploration and the thrill of the catch.

Sea Scape became the vessel through which I extensively explored the eastern United States coast, embarking on journeys up and down the coastline at least twice a year. These voyages were not just trips; they were explorations into the heart of the sea, each one an opportunity to connect with the water in a way that was both profound and personal. It was during these adventures that I penned *The Intracoastal Voyage of the Sea Scape*, a book that chronicled our travels and the myriad experiences we encountered along the way.

With a fuel capacity of 1,300 gallons of diesel, *Sea Scape* was designed for long distances, its range and stability unmatched. This capability allowed us to venture farther and with greater confidence than ever before, knowing that the vastness of the ocean was ours to explore.

Writing *The Intracoastal Voyage of the Sea Scape* was more than a recounting of adventures; it was an attempt to share the wealth of knowledge and experience I had accumulated over the years. I aimed to provide a resource that could guide others on their boating journey, offering insights and advice that could spare them the trials and errors that often accompany the pursuit of a passion. My hope was that this book would serve as a beacon, illuminating a path that others could follow toward their own dreams of life at sea.

Reflecting on the fleet of boats that had been part of my life, from the modest Grady White to the majestic *Sea Scape*, I realized that each vessel had contributed to my story in its own unique way. They were not just means of transportation; they were chapters in an ongoing tale of adventure, discovery, and love for the sea.

Sea Scape's odyssey, from a dream to a reality, was a journey of transformation, not just for the boat itself but for me as an individual. It was a testament to the power of dreams, the importance of perseverance, and the joy of sharing one's experiences with the world. As *Sea Scape* cut through the waves, it carried not just the physical weight of its passengers and gear but the hopes, dreams, and aspirations of a sailor who had found his calling on the water.

In the vast expanse of the sea, where the horizon stretches endlessly and the waves tell stories of adventure and discovery, I found my calling. My journey from a novice, battling seasickness and grappling with the complexities of boating, to becoming a seasoned sailor with a fleet of my own, has been both challenging and immensely rewarding. Along the way, I've learned not just about boats, but about life, resilience, and the pursuit of passions. It's these lessons, hard-earned and deeply cherished, that I feel compelled to share.

Boating is not just a hobby; it's a way of life. It offers an escape from the mundane, a connection to nature, and a platform for adventure. However, the path to becoming a boater is fraught with challenges, especially when it comes to purchasing your first boat. The sea of options, technical details, and financial considerations can be overwhelming, making the journey seem daunting.

With years of experience under my belt and a formal education in boating, I've navigated these waters, learning from each decision, mistake, and triumph. My fleet, ranging from nimble center consoles to the majestic *Sea Scape* catamaran, has taught me the importance of choosing the right vessel for your needs, budget, and dreams. This knowledge, gained not from textbooks but from the rolling decks of my boats, is what I wish to pass on.

This book, *How to Buy Your First Boat*, is a distillation of my experiences, designed to guide you through the intricate process of finding and purchasing your first boat. It's crafted to help you avoid common pitfalls and to illuminate the path toward making a decision that aligns with your aspirations, budget, and lifestyle.

Here, you'll find insights into

- understanding the different types of boats and their purposes,

- assessing your needs and matching them with the right vessel,
- navigating the financial aspects of boat ownership,
- the importance of a thorough inspection and trial before purchase, and
- tips for maintenance and long-term care of your boat.

More than just a practical guide, this book is an invitation to embark on your own journey of discovery. Boating opens up a world of adventure, offering endless opportunities to explore, relax, and connect with like-minded individuals. It's a journey that promises not just the thrill of the open water but also a deeper understanding of oneself.

"Enjoy and make a wise decision" is not just a piece of advice; it's a mantra for life. Whether you're dreaming of serene afternoons sailing along the coast or the adrenaline rush of racing across the waves, the right boat can turn those dreams into reality. This book aims to equip you with the knowledge and confidence to make that happen.

As you turn the pages, I hope you'll find not just information, but inspiration. May your journey into boating be as fulfilling and transformative as mine has been. Remember, the sea is not just a destination; it's a journey, and it starts with a single decision. Choose wisely, embrace the adventure, and let the winds of passion guide you toward your dreams.

Appendix A
CHECKLIST FOR BOAT INSPECTIONS

Exterior Inspection

- ✓ Hull: Check the hull for cracks, dents, or signs of damage. Look for any areas where the gel coat may be peeling or blistering.
- ✓ Keel: Inspect the keel for any signs of damage or wear, especially if the boat has been grounded.
- ✓ Bottom paint: Check the condition of the bottom paint. Look for areas where the paint may be worn away or flaking off.
- ✓ Propeller: Inspect the propeller for any damage or distortion. Check for any fishing line or debris wrapped around the propeller shaft.
- ✓ Through-hulls: Check all through-hull fittings for signs of corrosion, leaks, or damage. Make sure sea cocks operate smoothly.
- ✓ Anodes: Inspect the sacrificial anodes (zincs) for signs of corrosion or excessive wear. Replace them if necessary.
- ✓ Rub rail: Check the rub rail for any damage or missing sections. Ensure it is securely attached to the hull.
- ✓ Deck hardware: Inspect all deck hardware, including cleats, stanchions, and railings, for signs of corrosion or damage. Make sure fasteners are tight.

✓ Canvas: Inspect any canvas covers, such as bimini tops or cockpit enclosures, for tears, mold, or signs of wear.

Interior Inspection

✓ Bilge: Check the bilge for any signs of water, oil, or fuel. Ensure the bilge pump is operational.
✓ Electrical system: Test all electrical systems, including lights, switches, and accessories. Check wiring for signs of damage or corrosion.
✓ Plumbing system: Test all plumbing systems, including sinks, faucets, and toilets. Check for leaks or clogs in hoses and fittings.
✓ Fuel system: Inspect the fuel tank and fuel lines for signs of leaks, corrosion, or damage. Check fuel filters and replace them if necessary.
✓ Engine compartment: Check the engine compartment for any signs of oil or fuel leaks. Inspect belts, hoses, and connections for wear or damage.
✓ Steering system: Test the steering system for smooth operation. Check for any excessive play or binding in the steering mechanism.
✓ Throttle and shift controls: Test throttle and shift controls for smooth operation. Check for any sticking or binding.
✓ Safety equipment: Ensure the boat is equipped with all required safety equipment, including life jackets, flares, fire extinguishers, and signaling devices. Check expiration dates and condition.
✓ Documentation and paperwork:
✓ Registration and documentation: Verify that the boat is properly registered and documented with the appropriate authorities.
✓ Title and ownership: Confirm the boat's title and ownership history. Ensure there are no liens or encumbrances on the vessel.

- ✓ Maintenance records: Review maintenance records and service history to ensure the boat has been well-maintained.
- ✓ Warranty information: If applicable, review any remaining warranty coverage and transferability.
- ✓ Boat survey: Consider hiring a qualified marine surveyor to conduct a comprehensive inspection of the boat, especially for larger or older vessels.

Appendix B
GLOSSARY OF BOAT TERMINOLOGY

aft: The rear portion of the boat

anchor: A heavy object or device used to secure the boat in place by dropping it to the bottom of the water

ballast: Heavy material (such as lead or concrete) placed in the hull of the boat to provide stability

beam: The width of the boat at its widest point

bilge: The lowest part of the boat's interior where water collects and is pumped out

bilge pump: A device used to remove water from the bilge

boom: A horizontal spar attached to the bottom of the mast that supports the bottom edge of the sail.

bow: The front or forward part of the boat

cabin: The enclosed area below deck used for sleeping, cooking, and other accommodations

cockpit: The area of the boat where the helm (steering area) and controls are located

deck: The surface of the boat that you walk or stand on

draft: The depth of the boat below the waterline, measured from the waterline to the lowest point of the boat's keel or hull

helm: The steering wheel or control station on a boat

hull: The main body of the boat, below the deck, that floats in the water

keel: The structural beam or plate along the bottom of the boat that provides stability and helps it track straight in the water mast: A vertical pole or spar that supports the sails on a sailboat

port: The left side of the boat when facing forward

rigging: The network of ropes, wires, and hardware used to support and control the sails

rudder: A movable fin or blade located beneath the boat's stern that helps steer the boat

sail: A piece of fabric attached to a mast and boom used to harness wind power for propulsion

starboard: The right side of the boat when facing forward

stern: The back end of the boat

throttle: A control lever or knob used to regulate the speed of the engine on a powerboat

tiller: A handle or lever used for steering smaller boats

trim: Adjusting the angle of the boat's hull or the position of the sails to optimize performance and stability

Bass boat

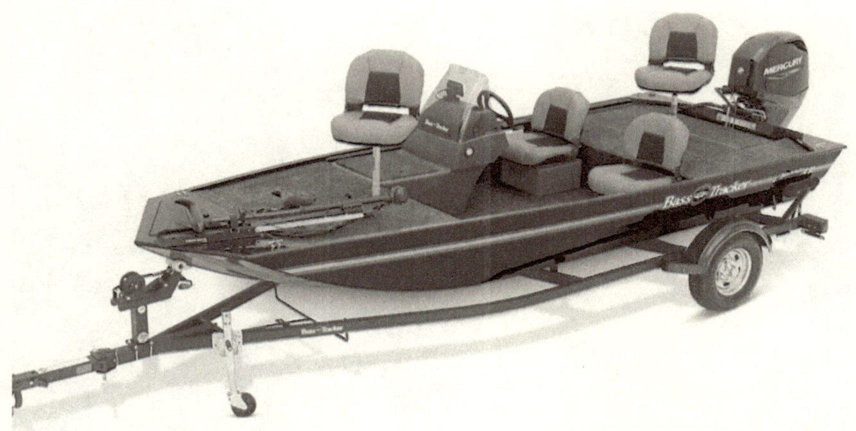

Center console

Sport fishing boat

Ski boat

Wake boat

Jet boat

Outboard Jet
Inboard Jet
impeller: Device used to pump and force water under pressure through a steering nozzle at the rear of the vessel
impeller
jet
intake grate: Screening cover over the intake, which prevents large debris from entering
intake: Opening in the hull that draws water toward the impeller
intake

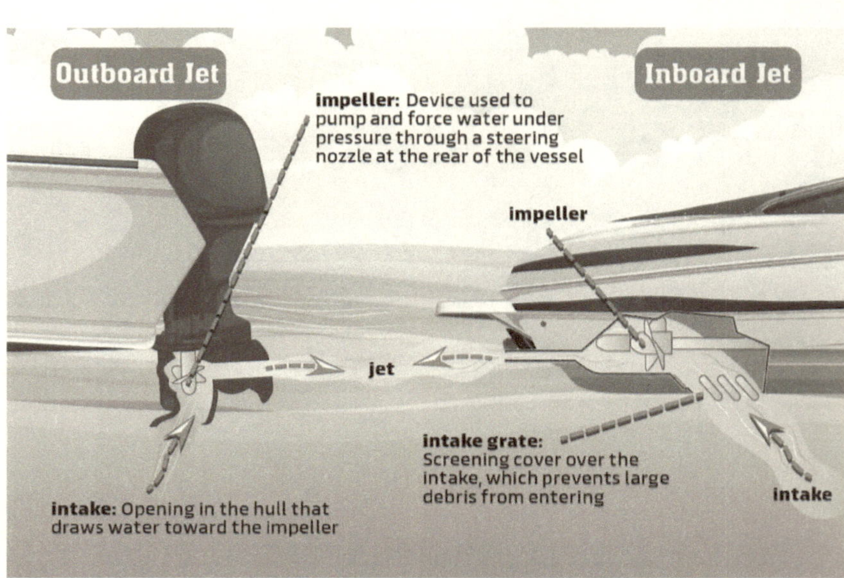

Dingy sailboat

Catamaran

Sailing yacht

Cabin cruiser

Motor yacht

Trawler

Speedboat

Sail racing boats

Pontoon boat

Kayak

Canoe

Rowing boat

Inflatable boats

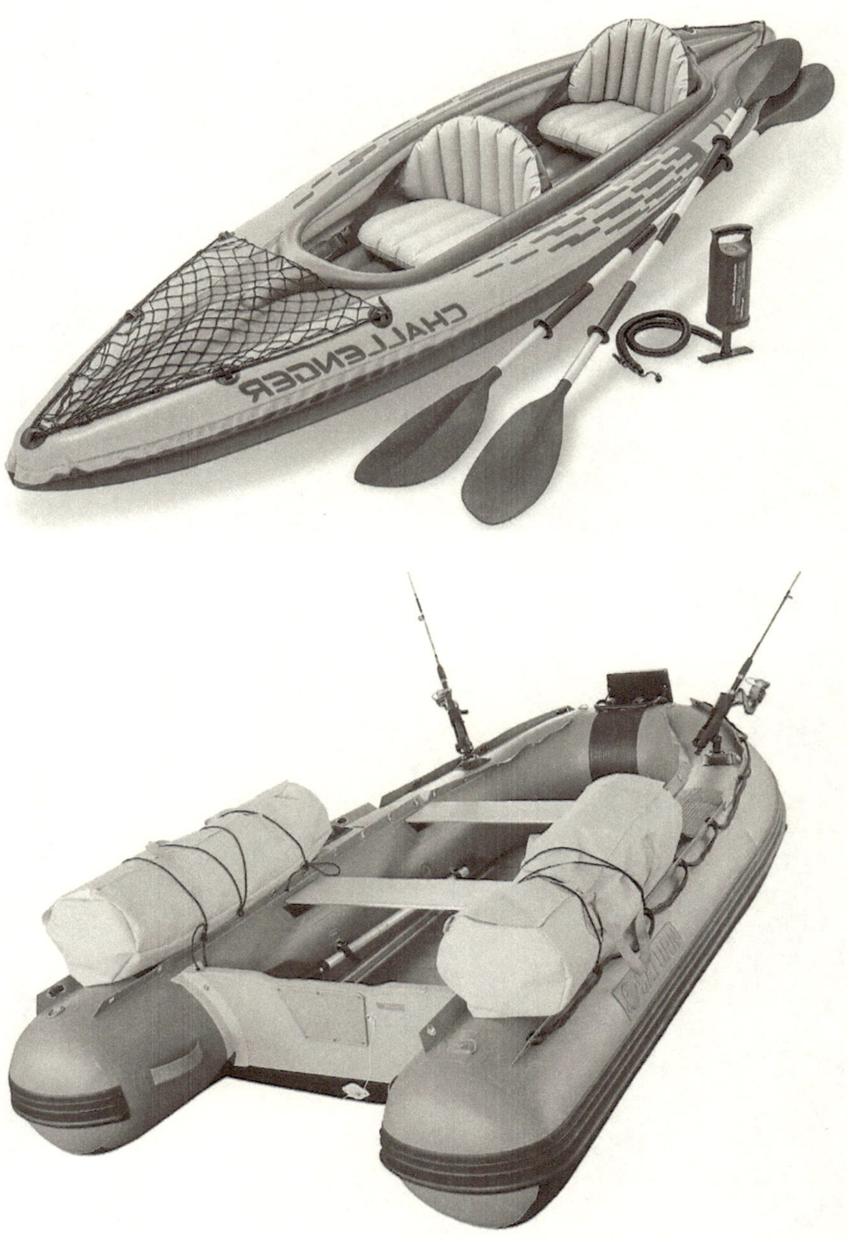

Mega yacht

Houseboat

Bibliography

Boatsetter Team. "Boating Inspection Guide: Things to Know Before Buying a Boat." April 19, 2021.

Wilson, Samantha. "The Top 15 Questions You Should Ask When Buying a New or Used Boat." October 2023.

Outdoor Recreation. "Understanding the Different Types of Boats: Which One Is the Right One for You." April 4, 2023.

Craig, Andrew. "How Much Does It Cost to Buy and Own a Boat: A Comprehensive Owner's Guide." Get My Boat Journal.

Herigstad, Sally, and Shepard, Dan. "How Much Does a Boat Cost? What You Need to Consider."

Rudow, Lenny. "The Cost of Owning a Boat: Budgeting and Financial Planning." Boats.com, June 14, 2018.

Boating World. "Costs of Boat Ownership: A Comprehensive Guide."

Roa, Sophia. "The 2023 Guide to Boat Storage." Sailing Cost.

Clane, James. "Boat Inspection Checklist: 31 Important Steps." Boatsgeek.

"Basic Boat Maintenance Checklist for New Boaters."

Strand, Rick. "Inspecting Your Boat's Finish: Imperfections in Your Boat's Finish Can Tell You About Its Structural Integrity." Boating, March 1, 2013.

Nicholson, Darrell. "Evaluating Marine Surveyors." Published: August 10, 2005. Updated: November 6, 2019.

Antill, John. "Creating a Mechanical Inspection Checklist." (Blog). September 21, 2023.

TheYachtMarket News. "11 Tips for Negotiating Price on a Boat." December 15, 2020.

Kalfrin, Valerie, and Tacher, Taryn. "Is It Too Low? What Is Reasonable to Offer Below Asking Price." August 14, 2023.

"Boat Financing: How to Secure a Boat Loan." Discover Boating.

Castillo, Juan. "Boat Insurance: An In-Depth Guide." June 17, 2016.

"Boat Transport Guide: Shipping Your Boat." Discover Boating.

Storgaard, Morten. "Boat Maintenance Checklist For Beginners (30 Important Steps)." Boating, General Boat Questions.

"Recreational Boating: Stay Safe on the Water."

"Boat US Foundation Courses on Safety."

"Safety Boating Safety Guide: Staying Safe on the Water." Discover Boating.

"Joining a Boating Club? Consider These Pros and Cons First." BoatingWorld.

"A Guide for Buying a Boat for the First Time." Progressive.

"First-Time Boat Buyers Guide: How to Buy a Boat." Nautical Ventures.

"Boat Buying Guide: What to Know Before Buying a Boat." Boat Care: Boat Tips and Resources, April 20, 2023.

"Boat Buyer Guide: Tips on How to Buy a Boat." Discover Boating.

Backman, Larry. "7 Questions to Ask Yourself Before Buying a Boat." October 7, 2022.

Ekman, Tom. "Boat Buying Guide 2023: Tips to Buying a Boat For First-Time Boat Buyers." Neighbor Blog, January 29, 2024.

"9 Things to Know before Buying a Boat: Your Guide to Boat Types, How to Buy, Insurance and More."

Burnham, John, and Wilson, Samantha. "How to Buy a Boat: The Ultimate Guide." Rightboat, May 3, 2023.

"Buying a Boat: A Complete Guide to Buying a Boat (with Checklists)." The Sailing Nomads.

"Steps to Buying a Sailboat." The American Sailing.

Stockdale, Paul. "A Complete Guide to Buying a Boat." March 15, 2023.

"Used Boat Buying Checklist." Van Isle Marina.

About the Author

Dr. Geffner's enduring connection to the ocean has been a steadfast presence throughout his life; it has allured his very existence. Even as he pondered the path to his postcollege life, the decision between delving into marine biology or medicine proved to be a challenging crossroad. His stint at Washington University School of Medicine in St. Louis, Missouri, though surrounded by an engaging environment and remarkable individuals, never detracted his heart's yearning to return to the coastal haven where he now lives with his family.

The early seeds of his seafaring affinity were sown during his childhood when his father introduced him to the world of sailing on Lake Hopatcong, New Jersey. Pursuing a degree in biology at Rutgers University in New Brunswick deepened his connection to marine life, as he had the privilege of working at the Sandy Hook Marine Laboratory in New Jersey, which was close enough in distance to the university. Armed with a bachelor's degree in biology and a master's degree in human anatomy from Rutgers, he then embarked on his medical journey.

Upon earning his medical degree from the New Jersey School of Medicine in Newark, New Jersey, he chose to stay close to home, completing a residency in internal medicine before venturing to Washington University School of Medicine, specializing in dermatology. He followed this degree with another in dermatopathology at Greensboro, North Carolina's Moses Cone Memorial Hospital, where, with their guidance and assistance, he obtained a degree in dermatopathology, which qualified his ability to interpret biopsies of the skin, a rare and sought-after qualification that garnered tempting offers from prestigious medical centers and other practices. However, the call to return home and establish his practice on the New Jersey shore, amidst the barrier islands, where he now resides with his wife, Patricia, proved irresistible.

While deeply engrossed in the medical field, providing life-saving procedures for his patients, his passion for boating, fishing, and sailing persisted unabated. Joined by his wife and fellow dermatologist, who grew up in Florida visiting the other half of their family, captured his heart and, as a result, prompted him to dock some of his other boats in Key West and Fort Lauderdale, where they are still there today. Presently, he relishes the company of his loving children—Victoria, Jonathan, and Julianne—residing in West Point Island, New Jersey, with his wife and him, merely four blocks away from the captivating expanse of the ocean. Fortunate and grateful, living on Barnegat Bay allows him the privilege of strolling a mere few blocks to the majestic ocean.

He has been very fortunate to have had a deep passion for the sea, and as a result, acquired a wealth of experience as a sea captain. Managing his fleet of boats over the years and dedicating himself to learning about the ocean has kept his passion alive. As a sea captain, he has encountered a variety of challenges and gained valuable insights into navigation, maritime operations, and marine biology.

Looking into the future, to keep himself updated, he plans to follow the latest maritime regulations and advancements in navigation technology and pursue additional certifications and obtain additional training to enhance his skills and credentials. With a growing awareness of environmental issues, he would like to explore ways to make his fleet more sustainable and environmentally friendly. This may involve adopting eco-friendly practices or even getting involved in marine conservation efforts. He would like to share his expertise with others who have similar desires and, when possible, mentor aspiring sea captains and contribute to publications that could make a difference. Sharing their experiences can contribute to the broader knowledge of the entire maritime community.

As a sea captain, he wants to stay abreast of technological advancements in the industry. Integrating the latest navigation tools, communication systems, and safety technologies can enhance the efficiency and safety of his fleet, as well as that of everybody else.

As a sea captain, he would like to explore new areas and embark on exciting maritime adventures with others. This not only keeps things interesting for him but could open up new opportunities and perspectives.

As a sea captain, he looks forward to engaging with his maritime community, both locally and globally, and he will always continue trying to attend industry events whenever possible connect with other sea captains, participate in discussions, and stay informed about industry's trends and challenges. The many opportunities that he has had have allowed him to explore and diversify his maritime endeavors. He hopes that his interest and passion will evolve to offering specialized services, such as marine tourism, research support, or even collaborating with scientific institutions. He has been most fortunate to be a scientist with a practice in dermatologic surgery and still be able to pursue his other passion. He cannot express the depth of his appreciation for having been able to do this with the help of his family and friends.